ESCAPE TO THE HILLS

Searching for the Simple Life in Rural Wales

By the same author

ESCAPE TO THE SEA

ESCAPE TO THE HILLS

Searching for the Simple Life in Rural Wales

Marie Wynne

Cover image:

A path leading to a forest. Snowdonia on a warm, sunny
August day and not a soul in sight. Peter Smyly, 2006.
Wikimedia Commons

For Owen

'Everything you have in this world
is just borrowed for a short time.'

Welsh Proverb

PROLOGUE

The cottage was perfect. True, it lacked some of the qualities of the cottage of my dreams, but I was ready to forgive it this. There were no roses scrambling round the wooden front door and the front garden was full of nettles rather than hollyhocks. Instead of the mellow brick of my imagination, this house was stone, its whitewash stark against the dark slate roof.

Disappointingly, the rough track we had followed across a rock-strewn field led not to a peaceful woodland glade or a sheltered hollow. Instead, we found ourselves at the top of a steep grassy slope. The wild landscape that rolled away before us was studded with gnarled oak and holly trees, huge strangely shaped boulders, and myriad tiny streamlets that glinted in the sunshine. And framing it all, dominating the landscape, were the mountains. Just the presence of a house in this windswept place, which seemed so uninhabitable, was almost a shock. I remember we both laughed out loud, feeling self-conscious in the stillness. Who would live all the way up here? You'd have to be crazy.

A high-pitched mewling had us craning our necks to scan what seemed like a vast sky. There they were: two buzzards circling lazily on the thermals high above the hillside. A soft breeze brought the scent of coconut from the yellow gorse flowers surrounding the cottage. We breathed in the cool fragrant mountain air and fell still. The place certainly had rural charm but, we agreed, living in such a remote spot full time would be impossible. Reluctantly we turned and began to head back up the slope.

'Look at that.'

To the right of the cottage, outside the little walled front garden, worn stone steps led enticingly into the shade of three ancient sycamore trees. We couldn't resist a little exploration before we left. The house was empty and even though we weren't going to buy it, a quick peek at the back garden would do no harm. Tumbledown drystone walls encircled a grassy wilderness. More familiar with concrete pavements, we stumbled laughing over soft hillocks of grass and earth. With fingers stained with wild blackberries, we stroked the glowing velvet lichen that covered the boulders of a small outcrop under the trees. We gazed at the soft-eyed cows in the water meadow behind the house and dabbled our fingers in a tiny pool half-hidden in a hollow.

Nature provides many types of enchantment but perhaps one of the most potent is that experienced by a child in a wild garden. That afternoon, in a neglected garden on a lonely hillside, we became children again. By the time we left the cottage we had fallen in love with the hillside.

A long six months later, we spent our first night in the cottage. We had bedded down on a futon mattress in front of the fire, the temperature upstairs too frigid to allow sleep. Tipsy on fresh night air, excitement, and a bottle of sparkling wine purchased hastily from the local shop, we had both fallen into a solid slumber. After months of wrangling, the cottage was ours. We had done what we had dreamt of for years: we had escaped the stress of the city and moved to the country. Yet despite my happy and relaxed mood, the vivid dream I had that first night was odd and unsettling. I dreamt of the two of us in our new cottage. But the dream house was very different to the real one. Somehow, the cozy little cottage had become a large rambling tower. It stood on a high conical hill. In the dream, we excitedly explored every nook of the tower, discovering a maze of spiral staircases and secret rooms. Eventually, we found ourselves at the very top of the tower, in a huge round room. Its many windows gave a 360-degree view of the landscape. But gazing eagerly out, my dream self was confronted with a dismal scene. There was no grassy slope, no tangled garden. The trees and mountains were gone. Instead, outside the tower walls, the steep hill fell away sharply. Far below the hill but surrounding it on all sides was a city. The lights, din, and smoke of this metropolis stretched as far as the eye could see. It was a scene that contained everything we had sought to leave behind. The rural idyll we thought we had found was just a tiny island amidst the encroaching urbanization.

In the morning, the uneasy mood the dream had generated dissipated as we contentedly busied ourselves settling into our new life. In fact, I quickly forgot all about it. However, like an unwelcome ghost, that strange dream and its disturbing atmosphere returned to haunt me with the events of later years.

1

As I sit writing this I am nursing a broken arm. I am struck by the irony that this period of enforced immobility has provided the perfect opportunity to plan and write this book. By a curious coincidence, our escape to the hills of North Wales was prompted by another injury, also of mine (yes, I am painfully aware of the lessons that need to be learnt here!). Identifying the significant events and turning points in the thread of one's life is perhaps more about weaving a story than plotting a series of facts. The stories we tell ourselves about our lives often change as we age, as if a longer perspective is needed to discover who we really are. Twenty years after moving to North Wales, we both agree that two things were responsible for our move: my knee injury and Julian Cope.

In April 1998, my husband Geoff and I flew to Dublin to present papers at a large academic conference, along with several colleagues from the university psychology department where we both worked. Outside of conference sessions, our little group walked miles exploring the sights, sounds, and tastes of Dublin. Sensibly, I had packed a pair of flat shoes suitable for walking. Unwisely, the shoes were new and I chose that week to break them in. My feet were blistered and my arches aching by the time we got home, but I was surprised when my left knee swelled up like a balloon. After my family doctor expressed bafflement, I consulted a joint specialist who diagnosed an unpronounceable tropical disease and glared at me disbelievingly when I insisted I had travelled no further than Dublin in the last twelve months.

A long three months later, after finally visiting an osteopath, I was diagnosed with a torn knee ligament caused by a fallen arch, and scheduled for a scan at a small hospital near Ruthin in North Wales. We decided to book time off work and make a day of it in Wales. We were both desperate for a break. Many people have a rosy image of academia as a tranquil life of study interrupted only by the occasional seminar in the pub. Popular representations of university life on television (and in many university prospectuses) usually feature dreaming spires, pretty quadrangles, and wildly enthusiastic students. While these images may resemble the experiences of university dons at Oxford and Cambridge in the 1930s, they are a very far cry from the stark reality of modern academia. The truth was that after almost ten years in the field, we both felt burnt out and disillusioned.

Like many universities, our own institution (which we affectionately called Colditz) had fallen victim to a trend for 'creative' management solutions that seemed mostly to involve changing the structure of the curriculum every three months and generating a mountain of new regulations. In the first semester of each year, we all ran around like headless chickens trying to get to grips with the changes. Once everyone had more or less become comfortable with the new system, the management changed it again. The more paranoid amongst us considered this new strategy to be strangely sadistic.

The university, we were now informed, was a factory, an industrial plant that must never shut down and must make as much money as possible. Thus, during term time, the university had to churn out the maximum number of students. During the summer, the campus was rented out to any organization bar Billy Smart's Circus (and probably only because Billy Smart refused to pay the ridiculously high rent).

We were under increasing pressure to produce as many research papers as possible, and quantity not quality was the watchword. The problem was that academia is not a 9 to 5 job, it is more of a vocation. Let's face it; there are much easier jobs that pay higher salaries and don't require a minimum of six years training. The desire to increase their knowledge and make original contributions to the field means that many academics never really switch off; there is always another book chapter or lecture waiting to be written, usually over the weekend. More and more, we were finding it impossible to juggle the ever-increasing number of tasks the job now required, and our family life and energy levels had suffered. It was a sign of how bad things had become that the prospect of a hospital visit was less stressful than going into work.

So that was how we found ourselves, one unseasonably hot April day, *en route* to Ruthin, a small characterful market town in North Wales. There has been much squabbling about the geographical and cultural boundaries of North Wales but it is generally agreed to comprise the northernmost parts of Wales. The region is bordered by England to the east and the Irish Sea to the west, and includes the island of Anglesey. North Wales was a Celtic stronghold against the invading Anglo-Saxons and Normans until the 13th century, when the area was subdued by the English. One reason why North Wales was often chosen as an escape is that the region is mountainous; it contains the wild landscape of the Snowdonia mountain range. In fact, Snowdonia and Anglesey were probably the last refuges of the Celtic Druids. Welsh identity and the Welsh language remain strong in Snowdonia. Although we were born in England, we both had Welsh ancestry. My family on my father's side was from the little town of Llanberis in Snowdonia. Geoff's family were mostly from the village of Hawarden, although a branch of the family originated in Ruthin.

I remember that day in Ruthin as being strange, almost dreamlike in some ways. As we left the city behind, the weather seemed to grow warmer and by the time we reached the countryside near Ruthin, it felt like midsummer. The car wound through narrow lanes bordered by lush hedgerows filled with hawthorn, cow parsley, and wild roses. The scent of wild garlic drifted through the open car windows. The unfamiliar names of tiny Welsh villages flashed past like some lost magical language: Efenechtyd, Melin-y-Wig, Llanarmon-yn-Iâl. We looked at each other. This was only an hour's drive from our home in Liverpool but it was like a different world.

In the hospital, we were directed to a featureless waiting room that looked out onto a courtyard garden. This opportunity to provide a welcome connection to nature in the sterility of the hospital had been wasted, as the garden contained a few cracked paving stones and three half-dead shrubs. After the scan was over, we emerged gratefully into the sunshine and drove into Ruthin. We wandered aimlessly through the little town, admiring the half-timbered houses and tiny antique shops. Over hot coffee and enormous tea cakes in a quirky little cafe, we congratulated ourselves on our decision to escape here for the day.

Suddenly, our chat was interrupted by a tremendous noise

from three motorbikes drawing up outside the cafe. Their leather-clad occupants entered noisily and took a table. But these were hardly Hell's Angels. The group consisted of a woman in her thirties with a young son, and a man and woman who looked to be in their mid-sixties. There was a strong family resemblance between the four. The man had a guitar with him and as the group sipped their drinks, he sang and played softly to his young grandson. We left the charming scene reluctantly and made our way back through the narrow streets to the car. Our route took us past a small estate agents and we couldn't resist a brief look in the window. Imagine living here! All the properties advertised seemed very expensive but we took a free property newspaper from a stand by the door before leaving.

We decided to drive back to Liverpool the long way, through Denbighshire. We had recently both become rather obsessed with neolithic monuments, and it was all the fault of Julian Cope. Two months earlier we had been to see The Teardrop Explodes singer at the Everyman theatre in Liverpool, where he was appearing as part of a tour for his book *The Modern Antiquarian*. The book is a large blue and orange tome that describes Julian's visits to many of the megalithic sites in the British Isles and expounds his lively theories of how these sacred sites were connected to the notion of the landscape as an earth goddess.

In the crowded auditorium of the Everyman, we listened as Julian, in platform shoes and leopard print coat, argued that modern society had led to a disconnection between people and the landscape, a sense of groundlessness that results in feeling disinterested and separate from the world. We watched delightedly as he gave a spirited impression of a gargoyle, squatting on the floor and howling at the plight of modern humans. It was a far cry from our usual diet of dry conference presentations and endless departmental research seminars, but much more enjoyable. In an odd way we both felt recharged by the end of the performance. What Julian said had resonated with us: we felt increasingly disconnected from the world outside academia.

So, on this strange hot day, instead of travelling straight back home we drove slowly through the country lanes to a small village called Llanarmon-yn-Iâl, accompanied by our copy of *The Modern Antiquarian*. There was a description in the book of an important prehistoric site just outside the village, an earth and timber motte or mound called Tomen-y-Faerdre. We found Llanarmon-yn-Iâl to be a tiny but pretty village with a circular churchyard, a pub, and a handful of houses.

In Welsh, the term *llan*, which features in many place names, means an area or settlement associated with a local saint. Thus *Llanarmon-yn-Iâl* means *St Garmon in the Yale* (an area of cultivated upland). We found the motte easily enough. Tomen-y-Faerdre is magical; covered with trees, it rises out of a beautiful lush landscape. Conscious of the fact that we had a long drive home, we allowed ourselves no more than half an hour to stroll round the base of the mound. But we had our book; we could return and explore this and other ancient sites. More importantly, our experiences that day in Wales—the landscape, the feeling of peace, the sense of reconnection—had strengthened the growing conviction that something had to change. We had to get out of the city.

2

There was little chance to think about Wales in the weeks that followed. The memory of our strange stolen day faded in the whirl of end of term exams and enormous piles of marking. We went to work, ate, slept, and repeated the process the following day. At the weekends we walked up to Camp Hill. The hill was only a short walk from our house in Woolton and was the site of an ancient hillfort. Of course, there were no signs of the fort now, and the tarmac paths and municipal planting did nothing for the place, but its big trees and grassy spaces were pleasant enough. And on really clear days, you could see the Welsh mountains.

In looking for our first house together, we had been drawn to Woolton because of its history and charm. This small suburb is one of the oldest in Liverpool. It is hard to describe exactly what we were looking for in that house-hunt. Ideally, we would have liked to move further out of Liverpool and into the countryside. In fact, I knew exactly where I wanted to live. On the bedroom wall in our rented flat I had put up a cheap print of my ideal home. I can't remember who the artist was but it was a twentieth-century painting of a bucolic country scene: a thatched cottage covered in roses and clematis, a picket fence, and a small front garden overflowing with herbs and summer flowers. Yes, it was a stereotype and it was the sort of style I normally hated, but for some reason I was drawn to the image and liked to imagine living there. A childhood spent reading *Swallows and Amazons*, *The Wind in the Willows*, and *The Famous Five* had created a longing for fields and woods to roam in rather than a plot on a housing estate. And both of us hated modern houses. We were agreed that our first house should be as old as possible.

Accordingly, we started house-hunting in the pretty little villages in Cheshire. I had long been bewitched by the writer Alan Garner's evocative descriptions of Alderley Edge. In Garner's novels, the hills, rocks, and woods of the Edge are full of enchantment. So, I was particularly keen to see if we could find a cottage in the village. However, Alderley Edge had become popular with footballers and soap stars and was well beyond our reach. After a few dispiriting weeks we reluctantly concluded that, despite our unhealthy attraction to old, rundown properties, we couldn't afford anything in the genteel countryside of Cheshire, and so we began searching in Liverpool.

Although technically still in the city, the house we finally bought in Woolton was ideal in many ways. It was Georgian and though neglected, still had lots of original features, such as a cellar with a small cast-iron range and beautiful original floorboards. Importantly, it had a small garden, which we had longed for at the flat. Although we weren't in the middle of the countryside, with a garden we could grow our own food and seek refuge from the stress of work. And we found that Woolton was rich in history. According to a local history book, a hundred years ago the people who lived in the houses on our road used to keep pigs in their front gardens. The discovery was strangely thrilling, although looking at our prim modern-day neighbours, we didn't think it was a practice that would ever return.

Despite (or perhaps because of) the cerebral nature of our jobs, we both felt a strong desire to grow things, to have a stronger connection with nature, and to do something other than spend every day in the office or lecture hall and every free evening in front of the television. In our rented flat, we had felt that something was missing from our lives. So we threw ourselves into renovating our neglected house and garden.

The garden was a typical urban rectangle of lawn that was about as inspirational as a wet weekend. The garden was on a slope, so Geoff used repurposed granite setts and old bricks to terrace it. We built a wildlife pond and four small raised beds for growing vegetables. The derelict shed at the bottom of the garden was replaced with a greenhouse and we filled it with tomato plants. In the house, we opened up boarded-up original fireplaces and installed a Rayburn range cooker, which transformed the kitchen with its warm presence.

We started making all our own bread. Hungry for more green space, we acquired an allotment, which allowed us to grow bigger crops like sweetcorn and squash. The allotment was only a few streets away from the house and provided some of the small-town camaraderie that we craved. Some of the allotment holders restricted their production to just one or two crops such as potatoes or peonies. But others seemed keen, like us, on becoming as self-sufficient as possible.

Access to the allotments was down a small lane that bisected a row of terraced houses, the gardens of which backed onto the allotment plots. The garden adjacent to our allotment had a fence separating it from the plot but there was a small picket gate in the fence. One evening we were working on the allotment when we heard someone hailing us. A woman was standing at the gate holding a tea tray. Over tea and biscuits, she told us that her father, who had recently died at a ripe old age, had worked not only our allotment but two others on different sites in Liverpool.

'He worked at the Liverpool docks,' she explained. 'But the work was irregular and we were always short of money. So he kept us going with food from his allotments; we always had plenty of fresh fruit and veg.'

She recalled slipping through the little picket gate, which her father had made, to join him on the allotment after school. She looked enviously at our rather rampant squash plants.

'Didn't you want to take over the allotment after your dad died?' I asked.

'Oh no,' she laughed. 'I haven't got time. Anyway, it's not really my thing.'

That evening we pondered what she had said. We were full of admiration for her father, who had managed to keep his family in food by working three allotments. We both worked full-time and strictly speaking, could afford to buy as much fruit and veg as we wanted to. And it was true that we had little free time. But we felt that growing our own food was important in ways impossible to explain. Working in the back garden or allotment had a sort of immediacy. It felt more real, more authentic, than most other things that filled our days. We could have gone to the local supermarket and bought summer squash, but we would have missed the joy of seeing the little squash seedlings sending out their strong tendrils at a rate of about a foot a day, and the beautiful squash flowers turning their faces to the sun. Worryingly, we were beginning to feel that the taste of a sun-ripened tomato fresh off the vine was more exciting than an overseas conference or a journal publication.

Although Woolton was a small community, there seemed to be little neighbourly exchange. The exception was Mrs Walton, an older lady a few doors down who had lived in the same house since she was a child. We became friends and she told us fascinating stories of what the village was like in the 1940s.

Our immediate neighbours were more difficult to get along with. At the bottom of our garden, a huge sandstone wall separated us from one neighbour. Some sections of the old wall badly needed repointing. Geoff decided to tackle the job himself and was soon up a ladder with a bucket of lime mortar.

I was watching him through the kitchen window while doing the dishes when I thought I heard voices. Then I saw Geoff rapidly descend the ladder. I went into the garden.

'Who were you talking to?'

Geoff was almost spitting with fury. 'That idiot over the wall!'

'Who?'

Apparently, our neighbour the other side of the wall had seen Geoff on the ladder and had come out to complain.

'What`s his problem?' I asked.

'He said ... he actually had the face to say that I was disturbing his privacy!'

I laughed. 'What did you say?'

'I pointed out what should have been bloody obvious to him: if the wall falls down through lack of maintenance he won't have privacy at all!'

'You should have mentioned his searchlight,' I said.

Our neighbour had a large motion-sensitive security light on the back wall of his house. Like a scene from the film *Close Encounters*, the bright light dazzled us every time we went into the back garden at night.

'If he's not careful, we'll give him something to complain

about,' Geoff said. 'We'll get some pigs for the back garden!'

It wasn't just the light pollution that began to bother us. In the three years that we lived there, the traffic through the village almost doubled. The village roads were narrow, their width suitable for horses and carts not motor vehicles. But at about 5 o'clock in the evening, most of the roads were gridlocked as people drove home from work. The road our house was situated on was one of the oldest in the village and had once been a track to the church. Geoff's mother worked as a nurse in a children's home in the village in the 1960s, and remembered walking in a torchlight procession to the church along our road. Now, lorries delivering to the local supermarket thundered through each day. The small front room was home to most of our books and a comfy sofa, and was a pleasant room in which to sit and read. But as the traffic increased, the honking of horns and the vehicle fumes filtered through the ill-fitting sash windows. We began to realize that we had been attracted to the Woolton of the past rather than the present-day modern village. We loved our house and garden and still liked the village. What's more, it wasn't that far from work. But it wasn't the rural idyll we had dreamt of.

Even our walks on Camp Hill became less satisfying. The hill was a good place to try and unwind, to dream, and to plot future projects. However, we had to cross two busy roads to get there. Even on the hill we could still hear the traffic, and our talks were usually interrupted by a council worker using a sit-on lawnmower or a deafening leaf-blowing machine. One of our favourite places on the hill was a little garden enclosed by a high stone wall. The garden contained several bright flowerbeds rather than the ubiquitous grass lawn. However, it seemed that every time we visited, another flowerbed had been grassed over to permit easier maintenance. We craved a bit of wilderness, a little more space. Nice as it was, the village wasn't providing it.

Things came to a head at Christmas, as they often do. It wasn't as if some kind of crisis occurred. In fact, we had spent an enjoyable day decorating the lounge with long tendrils of ivy, which grew in profusion over the sandstone walls that bordered the garden. We were looking forward to a break from work, and for once, there was no major work to do on the house or garden. We finally had the place as we wanted it. Now we could enjoy settling down after all our hard work.

That evening it started to snow. After a relaxing dinner, I went upstairs to draw the bedroom curtains. The snowflakes fell in gentle whirls, illuminated by the orange street light outside the window. It looked cold outside; the bare red and yellow branches of dogwood in the front garden were frosted. But it was warm and cozy inside. The Rayburn was running the central heating and a gentle warmth radiated through the house. I felt relaxed. Then, as I stared dreamily at the falling snow, a sudden realization struck. This house and everything in it wasn't really ours. It was owned by the bank and would be for the next twenty-five years until the mortgage was paid off. Of course, this wasn't a surprise; we had been happy enough to sign up for a mortgage to buy the house. But the enormity of the debt hadn't really struck me until now.

The knowledge that most people who bought houses did so with mortgages didn't reduce my unease. My thoughts kept going back to the fact that our current comfort and security depended on us being able to meet our mortgage repayments for years to come. And that meant we had no choice but to try to stay in our current jobs, or obtain similar ones. I wasn't sure I liked the sound of that. I had always assumed I would work in academia until retirement.

But the job was getting more and more stressful and we were both already feeling burnt out. What would it be like in a few years time? And we had twenty-five long years to go before we had paid the house off and could call it our own. Suddenly I felt trapped. The warm house, the tidy car on the driveway, the professional job no longer felt like achievements, they felt like burdens. This was not good, not good at all.

When I voiced my thoughts to Geoff he looked relieved.

'I've been thinking exactly the same thing,' he admitted. 'I thought I'd feel content once we'd found a house and were settled. But I don't.'

It was true that aspects of our city location weren't ideal, and it was a fact that we were becoming disenchanted with academia. But surely this was just what everyone felt? Life wasn't perfect. You had to make compromises and accept that you couldn't necessarily achieve all of your dreams. However, we both knew that our doubts were more than just cold feet at settling down. We shared similar adolescent memories of suburbia in the 1970s: regularly clipped lawns, orderly privet hedges, washing the car on a Sunday afternoon ready for the 9 to 5 to start again on Monday morning. We had both been inexplicably horrified by this lifestyle but here we were living it out. Just like all our neighbours, we climbed glumly into the car each morning and crawled back through the rush hour traffic every evening. The weekends were a mad rush as we raced to catch up with the housework, shopping, and laundry and fit in a few hours of relaxation. Of course, we knew we were lucky to be working in our chosen fields and to have a decent place to call home. And there was nothing inherently wrong with a lengthy mortgage and semi-detached normality. The problem was, we knew it somehow wasn't for us.

3

Our midwinter epiphany seemed to change nothing. Despite the heartfelt discussion about our sneaking sense of dissatisfaction with our lives, we carried on as normal. We had little choice; the winter term had started and we were so busy we had no time to think about anything other than work. Perhaps we would have continued along the same path indefinitely, burying our growing sense of unease under constant activity, if it hadn't been for that knee injury of mine. During that hot, dreamlike day in North Wales, one thing had become clear. What we were both yearning for was a different time, rather than a different place. Driving around Ruthin that day had been like stepping back in time. The sleepy country lanes, the hedgerows full of flowers, the quaint tea shops and old cottages suggested an older, more idyllic way of life that we both desperately wanted.

However, it was one thing to be seduced by a sunny day in the country and quite another to up sticks and move out there. The houses in the property newspaper we had brought back from Ruthin all seemed expensive. And the doubts we'd had about being tied into a mortgage hadn't gone away; did we really want an even bigger mortgage even if it could buy a house in the country?

I had put the property newspaper in the recycling pile and forgotten all about it until one Sunday afternoon, when I decided to sort through the pile. I found the estate agent's paper, now rather crumpled. I couldn't resist a last flick through. I looked longingly at pictures of beautiful barn conversions and Georgian manor houses, all with eye-watering price tags. Then, a rather small advert tucked away on one of the last pages caught my eye. There were only a few sentences of text and just one photograph. It showed the front view of a small, scruffy stone cottage. It was the kind of house a child would draw; indeed, the type of house I myself clumsily drew as a child. It was small and square, with two windows downstairs and two upstairs. Dead centre was a wooden front door surrounded by a stone porch. A short path led from the front door to a small picket gate. There was a large tree either side of the house, framing the picture. It was like a gingerbread house, I thought; a house in a fairy tale. When I looked at the price I drew in my breath sharply. It was only forty-five thousand pounds.

I practically dragged Geoff in from the garden to show him the details. When he saw the picture of the house his eyes lit up.

'And look at the price!' I said.

'Forty-five thousand,' he murmured.

We looked at each other. House prices had gone up considerably over the last three years. If we could sell, we might have enough left to cover half the cost of the gingerbread house.

'If we bought this,' Geoff pointed at the advert, 'we would have a tiny mortgage which we could pay off really quickly.'

I started to imagine what it would be like to be mortgage free, to own—to really own—this small portion of paradise and not have to work for ever.

'Whereabouts is this house anyway?' Geoff asked.

'Well, that's the funny thing. Look.' I pointed to the name of the village in the details.

'So?' Geoff looked puzzled.

'Well don't you think the name is really familiar? Like we've heard someone mention it recently?'

'No.'

I couldn't understand it. The name of that particular village had been bouncing around in my head all week and I hadn't been able to explain why. Geoff looked at me quizzically.

'It doesn't matter.' I shrugged. 'I must have heard the name on the radio or something.'

Over tea and homemade biscuits, we pored over the scant description of the property. The estate agents had been economical with details. The property, apparently, was in an 'outstanding' location in Snowdonia National Park. It had magnificent views and a water source.

'What kind of water source?' I wondered.

'Who knows,' Geoff said. 'Could mean anything from mains water to a puddle in the back yard.'

'Hmmm.'

We read on.

'Oh look,' I said. 'It says there is no proper vehicular access and no mains services.'

'Right,' Geoff said. 'So it is a puddle then. And a hell of a lot of work.'

'Might not be,' I said.

'It's got no electricity, no running water, and no proper sewage system,' Geoff pointed out. 'We'd have to be mad.'

He was right of course.

'Let's at least try to figure out where the village is,' I said.

I was trying to put off the inevitable: the moment when we admitted that the house was a crazy proposition and threw the newspaper in the recycling pile again.

We eventually found the village on a map. It was indeed in the middle of Snowdonia, not far from the small market town of Llanrwst and the pretty village of Betws-y-Coed.

'It looks quite far,' Geoff said doubtfully. 'Too far to commute.'

We gazed at the picture.

'It's so perfect,' I sighed.

'But would you really want to live with no power or water or anything?' Geoff asked.

I looked around our brightly lit kitchen. The gas-fired Rayburn was belting out heat and the aroma of the lasagne we had put in there earlier was delicious. I was looking forward to a hot bath later in our centrally heated bathroom. Could we give it all up to escape the rat race? Probably not.

By the time we had finished dinner we were in agreement. The gingerbread house was out. But the idea of finding a cheap rural property in need of work was appealing. We might have to settle for a small mortgage rather than being completely mortgage free. But it would be a step in the right direction.

Glancing round the kitchen before switching the lights off and heading to bed, my eye fell on the property newspaper, still open at the same page. I ran my finger over the picture of the cottage before carefully folding the paper and placing it in a drawer, well away from the recycling pile.

Over the next week, we both tried hard not to think about the Snowdonia house. It was too much work. And too far away. We needed a bolthole closer to the city because of work. But it would take time to find a rural house within our limited budget. And it was midsummer; things were busy in the garden and allotment and we didn't really have the time to start house-hunting. We resolved to do nothing until the autumn.

Then, on the Friday of that week, our resolve crumbled. We arrived home after an exhausting day. The weather was hot so the exhaust fumes in the road outside the house were awful. We had only just shut the front door behind us when there was a loud bang from outside, followed by lots of shouting. We raced back outside. The owner of a small hatchback with a dented bumper was yelling at the owner of a large Range Rover, presumably the cause of the dent.

This wasn't an unusual occurrence on our stretch of road. People got impatient with the slow-moving traffic at rush hour and got too close to the car in front. Although no-one was hurt, tempers seemed to have flared, perhaps because of the heat. The two drivers proceeded to try to yell each other down. The traffic came to a standstill and some of the other car drivers began to honk their horns and shout impatiently through their windows. Just when the two men were about to come to blows, a police car arrived and the situation began to defuse. We went back inside.

The road rage incident depressed us both. So much so that the next day, which was a Saturday, we decided to ignore the chores we had planned for the day and slope off to Wales.

'We could head for the Llanrwst area,' I suggested.

The estate agent handling the Snowdonia house was located in Llanrwst.

'We don't have to actually go in to Llanrwst,' I added hastily. 'It would just be interesting to check out the general area.'

'Of course,' Geoff agreed. 'We can just treat it as a little holiday.'

Naturally, we drove straight to Llanrwst and headed immediately for the estate agents. We easily found it; Llanrwst town centre was tiny. The small office seemed rather overstaffed; three women and a man raised their heads from their desks to smile at us as we entered. The man rose and came over to introduce himself.

'Hi there, I'm Gavin. Can I help?'

When we showed him the picture of the cottage we had cut out from the newspaper, he grinned and looked at us carefully.

'You do know the house has no mains services?'

We nodded.

'And you'd like more information?'

'We'd like to view the house,' I blurted out. 'Is that possible?'

Gavin raised his eyebrows and grinned again. His smile was infectious and we warmed to him.

'You'd really like to view it? Oh. Well, um, let's see now.'

He went over to his desk. The three women were watching us with unabashed interest, big smiles on their faces.

'Please, sit down, sit down,' Gavin said, looking a little flustered. He shuffled some papers. 'It couldn't be today, I'm afraid. I have a viewing in half an hour. And you see,' he lowered his voice conspiratorially, 'the ladies in the office don't like going up there. So it would have to be me.' He grinned again. 'We could arrange something for next week if you like?'

'That would be great,' Geoff said.

Gavin must have sensed our disappointment because he looked at us for a moment then retrieved a sheet of paper from a drawer.

'Look, if you like, you could go up to the cottage today and view the outside. It's empty at the moment, you see. Up to you.'

We agreed enthusiastically and Gavin handed us the sheet of paper, which contained what seemed like a lot of text and a small hand-drawn map.

'These are the directions. It's not far from here, but ... well, you'll see when you get up there,' he finished cryptically. 'By the way, what kind of car have you got?'

Mystified, we told him.

'Well, you'll have to leave the car at the bottom of the hill.' He pointed at a point on the map. 'Leave it just here. You'll have to walk the rest of the way. Without a four-wheel drive vehicle you won't get anywhere near the place except on foot.'

We thanked him profusely and took our leave, after arranging a full viewing for the following Saturday.

'Good luck!' he shouted as we reached the door.

One of the women giggled.

Before heading up to the house, we decided to find some food. Gavin's attitude suggested that we might need fortifying before attempting the trip, and the directions he had given us seemed hellishly complicated. A few doors down from the estate agents we were attracted by an old half-timbered shop, its windows full of antiques. It was the sort of place we both found irresistible, and so it turned out to be: three floors of cozy rooms stuffed with period furniture, bric-a-brac, and old shop mannequins sporting oddly put together outfits.

Happily, the shop doubled as a cafe, the entrance of which was guarded by a mannequin wearing a Victorian corset, 1970s flared jeans, and a bowler hat. Over good coffee and homemade cherry pie, served on antique china, we excitedly read over the directions Gavin had given us. The text mentioned several gates and the terms 'rough track' and 'unmarked lane' figured prominently, but with the optimism of the obsessed we were sure the estate agent had exaggerated the remoteness of the cottage.

Suitably refreshed, we headed out of Llanrwst, carefully consulting Gavin's map. After negotiating several unmarked lanes (and a few wrong turnings) we found what seemed to be the spot Gavin had indicated we should abandon the car and proceed on foot. Passing through two gates we found ourselves in a small wood on a rough rocky track. The track wound uphill under the canopy of ancient oak and beech trees. Brambles edged the path and bluebells peeped from the undergrowth. To our surprise, the trees petered out quickly and we emerged into a small clearing. It was windy up here, and the leaves on the few remaining trees rustled. Through the trees, we caught a glimpse of mountains. Beyond the clearing, the track disappeared and we found ourselves on an open hillside. There was nothing but grass and gorse as far as the eye could see, with an occasional drystone wall marking an unknown boundary.

'This can't be right,' I exclaimed. 'We must have taken another wrong turn. There's nothing up here!'

'It's got to be somewhere here,' Geoff insisted. 'The directions specifically mention this piece of woodland.'

After squabbling for a few minutes, we decided to explore a little further before admitting defeat and turning back. In the absence of any tracks, we followed the contour of the nearest drystone wall. Winding across the hillside, the wall ran underneath several twisted rowan trees and showed signs of being patched up in places. The hill was so quiet we found ourselves speaking in low voices, as if afraid to disturb the spirit of the place. As we rounded a corner, there was a clear view of the mountains. I caught my breath. The expanse of the Snowdonia mountain range stretched out before us: the Carneddau, Tryfan, like an ancient pyramid, and the gentle slopes of Moel Siabod. A shoulder of Snowdon was just visible behind Siabod. We felt like the last two people on earth. Even though we had failed to find the cottage, this view had made the journey worthwhile.

Then, just as we were thinking about turning back, we saw what looked like the corner of a slate roof above a grassy hillock. We quickened our pace, almost afraid that like a mirage, the image might disappear again. But then round the next bend, we came upon a small track bordered by trees. One tree, an ancient holly, showed signs of having been coppiced. The trees fell away as the track came to an end at a small rise. We fell silent. Straight ahead of us was a panorama that encompassed an almost endless hillside that fell away to a horizon filled with mountains and sky. In the foreground was the cottage. Seemingly rising out of the rock itself, the house squatted resolutely in the midst of this wilderness. Apart from the sheep scattering nervously out of our way, there was silence.

We lost track of time that afternoon. We looked at everything, drank it all in like people who had been starved of air and sky and trees. We peered through one of the small front windows but it was so dark inside we could make nothing out. We had better luck round the back. The tiny kitchen window, the sill of which was level with the ground, was partially broken, perhaps by the wind. We peered inside. The narrow kitchen was like a cave; the external walls were rough-hewn and followed the contours of the rock. There was a smell of damp and candle wax, and the floor was strewn with leaves that had blown in through the gap in the window.

On that afternoon, we observed and marvelled at the primitiveness of the house, at its simplicity and isolation. In our excitement, many other less charming characteristics escaped our notice, such as the fact that the house was built straight onto the rock (as evidenced by the huge boulders that constituted the base of the walls) and so had no damp proofing whatsoever. Or the fact that a herd of sheep wandered freely through the back garden, eating a wide range of invasive plants such as couch grass. We also failed to notice that there was no apparent drainage, source of water, or mobile phone signal. Blissfully unaware of these problems, we eventually found our way back to the car, tired and slightly windburnt, but thrilled. We hadn't even seen the inside of the cottage yet, but at that moment, if the house had been three times the advertised price we would have signed on the dotted line.

4

The euphoria of our pilgrimage up the hill and our first encounter with the cottage slowly faded in the following days. The car journey back from Snowdonia to Liverpool had seemed interminable. Did we really want a long commute twice a day? And then there was the whole prospect of off-grid living.

The day after our visit to Wales we had driven over to Chester for the afternoon. We had always liked Chester's attractive city centre with its mix of timber-framed buildings and niche boutiques and cafes. In one of the bookshops, we picked up a copy of *Hovel in the Hills*, Elizabeth West's lively account of moving to a remote cottage in North Wales in the 1960s. Ever the academics, we thought it wise to do a little research on the realities of living in the wilds of Wales with few amenities.

The book was both entertaining and horrifying. We loved Elizabeth West's humorous accounts of how she and her husband tried to renovate the neglected cottage they bought on a shoestring budget. However, her vivid accounts of battling with the elements on a windswept hillside were, quite frankly, rather worrying. It seemed that being responsible for one's own power, water, and waste was harder than we thought. And when we read how the West's collection of books gradually shed their covers because of the permanent damp in the cottage, we both baulked. We knew we could probably put up with being cold or short of cash but, bibliophiles both, we drew the line at losing our books.

By the time Saturday arrived, the day of the viewing, we had almost talked ourselves out of the move. The long journey back to Llanrwst did nothing to dispel that mood. We had arranged to meet Gavin at the spot where we had left the car the week before and to trek up the hill together. The draw of the landscape was as powerful as it had been at our previous visit; after a stressful week in the city, we breathed in the mountain air like it was a drug. On the small rise just above the cottage, we all stopped to gaze at the mountain view.

'I bring my family up here for picnics sometimes,' Gavin told us.

'Aren't you tempted to put in an offer for the house?' asked Geoff.

'Oh good grief, no!' Gavin said. 'My wife would never live up here! But this hillside ... well, it's the nicest place I know. Sometimes I come up here on my own at lunchtimes. Just to relax a bit, you know?'

We did.

After showing us in and pointing out one or two features, Gavin wandered around outside while we explored every inch of the cottage. The smallness of the place was a shock. Our current house wasn't large, but it was Georgian and more generously proportioned. The thick wooden front door of the cottage led into a tiny hallway with a small staircase. Off the hallway was the dark kitchen we had peered into the previous week. It contained a chipped Belfast sink. So the house did have water! This was cheering. However, on closer inspection, we saw that the water system was alarmingly primitive. The water seemed to be fed from a small plastic water tank which sat under a slate shelf in a corner of the kitchen. Fixed to the wall above the sink was an old-fashioned calor gas water heater which had seen better days.

'But how is the water pumped to the heater?' Geoff wondered aloud.

A quick search located the power source for the pump. Directly under the sink, open to any accidental splashes of water, was an old car battery. We looked at each other. It was a far cry from our comfortable kitchen at home.

A small sitting room was the only other room downstairs. This was larger than the kitchen but about a quarter of the space was taken up by the largest inglenook fireplace we had ever seen. If you ducked your head under the thick mantelpiece you could easily stand up in the fireplace. By contrast, the fire grate itself was very small. If that was the only source of heating in the house, then it would be very cold indeed. There was a motley collection of musty-smelling books on the mantlepiece. I selected what looked like an old poacher's handbook but hastily put it back when it almost disintegrated in my hands. So Elizabeth West had been right about books shedding their covers. It wasn't a good sign.

We made our way up the stairs, which led directly into the smallest of the two bedrooms; there was no doorway. This room housed a battered armchair, an old chest, and a portable loo of the type found in caravans. Evidently there was no bathroom in the house. The other bedroom was a little larger. This room was directly over the sitting room and the large chimney breast ran up one wall. Despite this, the room smelt damp. A single bed had been pushed up against the chimney wall; we noticed that the headboard of the bed had a light dusting of mould. We went to inspect the small sash window. There was a graveyard of dead flies on the wooden windowsill and a large yellow damp stain on the wall under the window. But the view of green hillside, trees, and distant mountains was magnificent.

Back downstairs, we quizzed Gavin about the house's history and structure. How old was the house? we wondered. Did the current owner live here all year round or just in the summer? Gavin either didn't know or wasn't telling.

We made our way back to the cars and took our leave of Gavin, promising to be in touch. Before the trip, we had decided to make a weekend of it and stay overnight in the area. An Internet search had revealed several bed and breakfasts nearby, one in the village itself. The village was tiny, and seemed to consist of a pub, a church, a bus stop, and a handful of houses. A sign outside the pub advertised food. We decided to try and find the bed and breakfast, which apparently was a farmhouse. It would be fun to stay in the village and get a feel for the area while we tried to get our thoughts in order.

The late afternoon light was mellow as we drove down the narrow lane. We easily located the farmhouse, which was a short walk from the pub. We parked in the farmyard and made for the house, which was a large stone and slate construction with several ancient outbuildings. Before we could knock on the front door, a figure emerged from one of the outbuildings.

'Mr Roberts?' we enquired.

The farmer stopped in his tracks, startled at our presence. We guessed he was in his late seventies.

'Are you Mr Roberts?'

The man took off his flat tweed cap and fiddled with it nervously before nodding reluctantly. We introduced ourselves and asked whether he had any rooms available that night. Mr Roberts looked panicked.

'Going to Chapel,' he finally said. 'Won't be back until seven.'

We looked at each other, unsure what this portended. Did going to Chapel rule out the possibility of accepting guests or were we just expected to come back later? Luckily, at that moment the farmhouse door was flung open and a short determined looking woman emerged.

'Euan!' she exclaimed. 'What are you doing?'

Slightly nervously, we explained who we were and what we wanted.

'Bed and breakfast is it?' she said in a tone of wonderment. 'Well I never!'

We guessed that the Robertses didn't see many guests.

Quickly recovering herself, Mrs Roberts was soon ushering us inside the house.

'Well of course we have a room, a nice room ... Euan!' she yelled over her shoulder, almost deafening us. 'Fetch some more milk!'

Mrs Roberts led us into a rather formal front room filled with furniture that looked too large for it. A forest of family photographs was on display on top of a huge dark wooden sideboard. She smoothed the embroidered tablecloth that covered the dining table and urged us to sit. When she produced two linen napkins from a drawer in the sideboard, I said, 'Oh, please don't go to any trouble. We weren't expecting a meal.'

'But you'll be taking tea and bara brith?' she said.

We knew a rhetorical question when we heard one and nodded meekly.

Mrs Roberts served strong tea with milk from the Robertses own cows. Her homemade bara brith (or 'speckled bread') was delicious; a firm dark fruity tea bread popular in Wales. Over tea, she plied us with questions and we owned up to our interest in the cottage on the hill. She looked astonished and a little disapproving that we might want to buy the cottage. When she found out we were vegetarians during a conversation about local food, she screwed up her face, pursed her lips, and said nothing.

In the local pub that evening, we laughed about the conversation over a beautifully cooked vegetarian lasagne and a bottle of surprisingly good house wine.

'I think she might have forgiven us for our interest in the cottage if we hadn't been vegetarians,' I said.

'I know, but at least it stopped her insisting on cooking us dinner,' Geoff said. 'She looked almost overjoyed when we said we were heading to the pub for food.'

Over dinner, we discussed the cottage. We both admitted that the viewing had only increased our doubts about the place. Yes, the location was beautiful and unique and the cottage was not without charm. But it was small and primitive and would be a hell of a lot of work. And it was hardly the sort of place you could ask builders to work on; it would be hard enough even getting shopping up to the house, let alone building materials. Anything that needed doing to the place, which was basically everything, would have to be done by the two of us. It was true that the Wests had renovated their cottage with no outside help, but they hadn't had a long commute and full-time jobs in academia. Did we really want to become part-time peasants? The more we discussed it, the more the prospect of actually leaving the city and moving up here seemed preposterous.

By the time we left the pub for the short walk back to the farmhouse, we had more or less agreed that the whole venture was impractical and that the place wasn't for us. But we could enjoy what was left of the weekend before heading back tomorrow to so-called civilization.

We strolled down the little lane through the village. Creamy blooms of cow parsley spilt from the hedgerows. The dusk had turned the mountains pink. Apart from the muttering of small birds settling down in the trees and hedgerows, there was silence. There was no traffic on the lane and we took a childish pleasure in walking in the middle of the road, city-dwellers released from our fetters. We felt free.

Back in our pretty bedroom, we drank tea in bed then fell into a deep sleep, lulled by the mountain air and the lowing of sheep. In the morning, refreshed and relaxed, we watched the graceful comings and goings of the swallows who had nested in the eaves just above our window. We were a little trepidous about facing the formidable Mrs Roberts over breakfast and hoped we wouldn't have to offend her by turning down homemade sausages. But she surprised us by a sunny smile and a magnificent, and meat-free, breakfast.

When we had finished, she stood over us and boomed, 'So! We'll be neighbours then!'

And we, despite resolving the night before to walk away from this mad adventure, we sat there and smiled and nodded, like fools under a spell.

5

The next morning, we called Gavin and told him we wanted make an offer on the cottage. He was pleased, but warned us that the sellers had had several very low, 'silly' offers and were holding out for a higher amount. Although we felt that forty-five thousand pounds was a reasonable asking price, the cottage needed a lot of work. And the whole idea was to end up with as small a mortgage as possible, or the venture would not be worth it. To our relief, our offer of forty thousand (subject to survey of course) was accepted.

We drifted through the next few days in a state of relaxed contentment. At work, I found myself staring out of windows dreamily, my head full of fields and mountains. I was brought abruptly down to earth when we tried to arrange a survey. A building society we had approached about a mortgage had given us the names of five surveyors. Three of them flatly refused to survey the house, because of its age, tumbledown condition, and lack of decent access. The fourth told us that he had already surveyed it for another potential buyer and he believed the house wasn't worth what we had offered for it. However, he did provide us with the name of another surveyor who he said might take on the task. He also warned us that, given the location, we needed to find a surveyor who was fit and healthy, had a four-wheel drive vehicle, and had someone to help them with ladders. We got the impression that he hadn't enjoyed his trek up to the cottage.

Wearily, we phoned the number he had given us. With a name like Medwyn Jones, the surveyor was obviously Welsh, and we hoped he would be a little more sympathetic to the property and its location.

The phone was answered by a cheery sounding woman who turned out to be Medwyn's wife.

'Oh he can't do it this week, dear,' she said in response to my enquiry. 'He's away at the Eisteddfod!'

Medwyn had a marvellous voice, his wife told me proudly. Apparently he sang at the Eisteddfod, a Welsh festival of music and song, every year. She promised to ask him to call. He phoned a week later, and we were relieved when he agreed to survey the house. When we explained about the difficult access, Medwyn seemed unfazed.

'Some of the locations I've been to in this job would make your hair stand on end!' he said. 'Don't you worry about me; I'll take my flask with me and I'll be as right as rain!'

'Do you think he meant his thermos flask or his hip flask?' I asked Geoff.

'Don't know, but I suspect he's going to need both!'

Two weeks later, Medwyn called to say that he had completed the survey and had mailed his report to us. He said he had thoroughly enjoyed his trip. He declared that the cottage was 'unique' and the location 'outstanding.' However, the place had been a little less isolated than he had expected. Apparently he had marched up the garden path to be confronted by a pair of knickers drying on a makeshift washing line. Giggling, he told us that when he had let himself into the house, he had found the owner in bed upstairs.

'I think I gave them a proper shock!' he guffawed.

Despite waxing lyrical about the 'fascinating vernacular style' of the house, Medwyn pronounced it virtually uninhabitable. He pointed out the extensive damp, the dodgy roof, the lack of sanitation, and many other problems. I was tempted to quip, 'Apart from that, it's okay is it?' but resisted.

'And then there's the vermin,' he concluded.

'Vermin?' I repeated.

'Rats, I mean,' Medwyn announced, with obvious satisfaction and a lovely Welsh rolled 'r'. 'Lots of them.'

It was my turn to be unfazed.

'Oh they won't bother us,' I said. 'We like animals.'

There was an astonished silence from Medwyn. Then, recovering himself, he guffawed. 'I suppose as long as you get yourselves a few cats you'll be alright!'

When Medwyn's report arrived, it was so thick it looked more like an encyclopaedia than a survey. The general tone was doom-laden and there was a special section on vermin and other natural threats to the fabric of the house and its inhabitants. As a guide to the work that needed to be done on the house, it was horrifying. As a bargaining tool, it proved to be invaluable. Medwyn stated in no uncertain terms that the house wasn't worth a penny over thirty thousand pounds.

We phoned Gavin and made a revised offer.

'I'll tell the owner,' he said. 'But they may not accept. Another couple are interested in the property.'

Our hearts sank. The other potential buyers hadn't yet made an offer, we learnt. Apparently, they wanted to arrange a mains electricity connection to the house. We felt something close to outrage. The hill was a special place, a sanctuary away from modernity and all its distractions. The cottage was a rarity, a place that had somehow escaped modernization and offered a taste of an older, more authentic way of living. We felt it would be a sacrilege to destroy its character and turn it into some kind of twee version of a holiday cottage.

During our walks on Camp Hill, we fretted about the possibility of losing the cottage. We tried to be philosophical but spiritually we had already made the move. Having glimpsed an alternative life, the prospect of staying in the city and plodding away at work seemed intolerable.

After a stressful couple of weeks, Gavin called to tell us that our offer had been accepted. We were jubilant. To our surprise, Gavin was too.

'I wanted you two to have it,' he said. 'I know I should be impartial, but I don't like the idea of the place changing. I know you two love it the way it is.'

We suspected he was referring to the potential buyers who had enquired about connecting the cottage to the grid. What other changes had they wanted to make? In fact, we heard some time later that they had been quoted fifteen thousand pounds for a mains connection, so it was perhaps unsurprising that they had walked away from the project.

Either way, we were just happy that the cottage was going to be ours. Assuming of course that we could raise the money. We had accepted an offer on our Liverpool house, but after repaying the mortgage we would have only eight thousand pounds left, and so would need to borrow twenty-two thousand. We felt sure that such a small mortgage should be easy to obtain. We were wrong.

We first tried a large building society with ecological credentials. We were going to be living off-grid and renovating the house using natural materials. However, after initially making positive noises about the project, the building society declared that the project would 'not be green enough' for them to support us. As they didn't elaborate on which green standards we had failed to live up to, we gave up and approached a more traditional building society.

We spoke to a friendly agent called Pamela. Well-groomed and crisp in a stylish skirt suit, she gushed over the photographs we showed her of the cottage.

'Oh, it's dead romantic!' she declared. 'I'm so jealous!'

We seriously doubted this; a primitive dwelling in the middle of nowhere didn't seem Pamela's style at all. However, we were grateful for her enthusiasm. We discussed our plans for the place: a compost toilet, solar panels, and wind turbines. Pamela smiled politely but we could see she was out of her depth.

'But these ... these ... woodbines ...'

'Wind turbines,' Geoff corrected her.

'Oh yes ... them ... how do they work again?'

The more information we gave Pamela about the cottage, the more doubtful she looked. As her perfectly manicured fingers turned the pages of Medwyn's report, we sensed we were losing her.

We were right. The building society agreed to give us a mortgage for the twenty-two thousand pounds, on condition that all the work on the house was completed first. As we estimated that this would take about 15 years (and a lot of money we didn't have), we turned down their offer.

We tried several other lenders with no luck. We began to realize that those aspects of the place that we considered assets, such as the house's uniqueness, the wonderful location, and the opportunity for off-grid living, the lenders saw as liabilities. Even our solicitor tried to warn us off. He read Medwyn's survey report with horror. When we tried to describe what a unique opportunity we thought this was, he shook his head.

'You'll never be able to sell this house again,' he declared. 'No-one else would want to live there. I wouldn't.'

He almost shuddered as he gazed at the picture of the cottage on the estate agent's details. 'I like my home comforts.'

We replied that we would never want to sell it, so the issue was academic.

'Well,' he concluded. 'I'll be surprised if you manage to get a mortgage on it.'

We gave up applying for mortgages and desperately started ringing round loan companies to try to raise the money. But time and again we got the same negative response; apparently you could get a personal loan to improve, extend, or otherwise prettify your home, but not to actually purchase a home.

Then we struck lucky. We picked up a leaflet in our local supermarket offering personal loans. I called the same day to enquire, holding out little hope. I admitted that the loan was to buy a house.

'Oh that's fine,' the operative said.

I nearly dropped the phone in astonishment.

'Are you sure?' I asked. 'It's okay to buy a house with the money?'

'It won't be a problem,' she said. 'I'll put the forms in the post today.'

We weren't sure if this particular supermarket just had more liberal lending rules or if the operative just didn't care as long as we signed up to the loan. But when the forms came we signed them and sent them off by return of post before the lender changed their mind.

We celebrated by taking a trip to Wales. That year, there was a full solar eclipse. What better place to view it than up at the cottage? However, someone else had had the same idea. Parked by the track leading to the cottage was a rather battered Land Rover. A man was sitting on the bonnet watching the sky. We guessed that it was the cottage's owner. Anxious to avoid any awkwardness, we pretended we were just two walkers out for a stroll on the hill. We walked purposefully past the Land Rover, exchanging a polite hello with the man. Disappointed that we couldn't visit the cottage, we kept on walking until we were out of earshot and then climbed up the hillside to get a good vantage point.

'You can't blame him for wanting to be here,' I observed. 'I feel sorry for him, having to shortly leave this place. I could never leave.'

As the light fell, the hillside was enveloped in a strange hush. Even the gentle munching of the sheep stopped. As the colour leached from the landscape, we were left in an unearthly world of dusky forms: rock, mountain, tree. As the light gradually returned and the birds resumed their song, we lay on the hillside and gazed up at a lightening sky.

On the way back, we visited a nearby neolithic site we had read about in Julian Cope's book. The track to the site lay through a farmyard and across a field. The farmer returned our greeting but watched us carefully to make sure we shut the farmyard gate properly. Trekking across the field ahead of us was another couple on their way to the site. One of them was clutching Julian's book. Geoff laughed.

'I bet farmers all over Wales are muttering to themselves, "That bloody blue and orange book again!"'

6

As psychologists, we were fascinated by the reactions of our families, friends, and work colleagues to our prospective move. Their responses ranged from envy to barely concealed horror. Our families thought that we were crazy, and were concerned about our safety and welfare living 'in the wilds.' They were astonished that we planned to leave a comfortable house in the city for a cold stone cottage with no facilities. Geoff's mother gazed at our gleaming Rayburn and exclaimed, 'But you've only just put this in!' My father, who hated the cold, was shocked that we would buy a house with no central heating. Almost everyone pointed out the negative aspects of the move, the things we would have to leave behind or might miss. We were continually asked 'But what will you do without ...?'

We were interested to observe that people's main worries tended to reflect their own particular concerns. My mother asked what we would do without an iron or ironing board. My father fretted that we wouldn't be able to call for help without a phone signal. When we told my sister that we would have no television, her mouth literally dropped open. The well-turned out secretary at work was horrified that we wouldn't be able to run a washing machine, and a friend who worked online from home enquired how we thought we were going to run a computer with no mains power. Almost everyone was horrified that the cottage had no bathroom, and more than one person anxiously enquired if we would have a toilet installed by the time they came to visit.

Many people expressed concerns about the isolation of the cottage. One of our friends, who was rather an anxious type, asked in all seriousness, 'But what about axe murderers?' and seemed surprised at our laughter. Two friends whose marriage was going through a difficult patch pleaded with us to consider whether our relationship was strong enough to withstand the rigours of life on a remote hilltop. We recognized their concern for what it was: a perfect example of the psychological projection of their own state onto us.

'I can see why they're worried,' Geoff said after our friends had left. 'If they moved into the cottage, they would probably kill each other within forty-eight hours!'

But the reactions of some of our work colleagues were strange. They seemed almost angry that we were moving away from the city and trying to break free of the rat race. Then it dawned on us. We had challenged the common assumptions that one had to work hard (extremely hard) to climb the career ladder, obtain the trappings of success, and generally accept the limits of working within the system. If you wanted to get on, you didn't challenge those basic assumptions.

Perhaps our desire for freedom stirred a similar chord in some of our colleagues, but they felt they couldn't make the break. Our line manager, who was wedded to his job, questioned us particularly closely about how far away the cottage was. We sensed his disapproval at our desire for something other than work. We suspected we were breaking an unwritten rule that staff should structure their home life around the job, not the other way round. It was acceptable to visit the wilds of the countryside for a holiday (booked well in advance and only during those weeks of the summer specified as academic holidays by the management), but not to actually go and live there.

But we didn't want part-time beauty: spending every week wishing for Friday and then racing over to North Wales at the weekend for some respite from the madness. We didn't want to work for forty years and spend our money on holidays to assuage an inner emptiness. We wanted a more meaningful existence now. We wanted to live in a place that fed our souls and inspired our imaginations. Then we wouldn't need holidays or any of the other trappings that most people use to try and paper over the cracks.

Once they got over the initial shock, most of the people who knew about our plans confided that of course they would love to do the same if only they were younger, richer, braver, fitter, etc. We tried to explain that what we were doing didn't require any specific qualities other than a burning desire to escape. But we sensed in many people, even those who thought we were mad, a kind of vicarious excitement. It was as if our outlandish decision had released something in them, a sense of possibility and freedom.

The day finally arrived. We moved into the cottage on the day before Christmas Eve. A few days before, we drove to Betws-y-Coed with a list of essentials we knew we would need to cope with our new primitive living conditions. In one of the outdoor supply shops we found a portable toilet of the type used in caravans. We had decided that this would be the best short-term solution; we could figure out a more satisfactory arrangement once we were settled. We also bought a selection of outdoor clothes and some walking boots. Our tidy urban wardrobes were ill-suited to a windy, muddy hillside and a lack of proper laundry facilities.

From one shop, we bought flashlights, head torches, a selection of battery-operated lanterns, a camping kettle, and a stash of batteries. With the end of the millennium approaching, the newspapers had been full of speculation about Y2K problems such as power cuts and computer outages.

Tilling up our goods, the shop assistant asked us nervously, 'Do you know something we don't?'

We just smiled. Little did she know that the power shortages we were about to face had nothing to do with Y2K.

The day of the move was cold, with a frost promised for that night. We had sold our car and bought a second-hand Jeep with off-road tyres. It was an expense we could have done without, but it was essential given the terrain. There was no chance of getting a removals van anywhere near the house, so we took with us only what we could transport in the Jeep. The back seats were crammed with bags of clothes and personal belongings, and our two cats. We had dismantled our wooden bed and sofa and tied these to the top of the Jeep. We only hoped the rather precarious arrangement could withstand the bumpy ride up the track to the cottage.

We had arranged to pick up the keys from the owner's sister, who lived near the Welsh border. We drove there through small flurries of sleet which we hoped wouldn't turn into proper snowfall before we got up to the house. After several wrong turns, we finally found the correct road, which was on a monstrous labyrinth of a modern housing estate. Many of the houses had Christmas lights twinkling in the windows or festooning trees in the garden.

But one house stood out from the rest. It was smothered in Christmas lights of all shapes and colours and shone like a gaudy beacon in the gathering dusk. Almost every tree in the front garden was similarly lit, and in the centre of the lawn, taking pride of place, were two lifesize wire reindeers that flashed and sparkled. We looked at each other open-mouthed.

'You don't think this is the house, do you?' Geoff said.

'Oh please let it be,' I prayed. 'It would be so perfect if it was this one!'

It was. A middle-aged woman answered the door. After a few pleasantries, she handed us a small bunch of battered keys and explained which was which. She followed us down the driveway to the Jeep. When she saw the furniture tied on top, she exclaimed 'I didn't realize you were moving into the cottage today! Are you going to spend Christmas there?'

We nodded.

She grinned. She clearly thought we were mad. We glanced behind her at her modern box of a house with its acres of fairy lights. As far as we were concerned, she was the crazy one.

By the time we reached Llanrwst it was almost dark. We had hoped to drive up to the cottage in daylight, as this was the first time we had taken the Jeep up there. However, by the time we reached the clearing in the wood, the light had fallen. A pale crescent moon provided little light. It was dark; really dark. The Jeep's headlights provided the only artificial light. I switched them full on to help Geoff, who was struggling with the stiff lock on the last gate. Alone in the car, apart from the mewling cats, I watched the trees swaying, for a brisk wind had risen. I hoped the ties would hold the furniture on the roof until we got to the house. On the way up through the woods a sofa leg had caught a couple of overhanging branches, which had almost had the whole lot off. It then hit me for the first time. On a dark, cold night we were about to move into a cottage with no lights, no central heating, no cooking facilities, and no bathroom. What had we done?

In the morning, my fears had vanished. We hadn't bothered to try to assemble the bed or sofa in the gloom; we had just bedded down on a mattress in front of the fire and fallen asleep immediately. I could hear Geoff breathing quietly next to me as he slumbered. I lay there and grinned to myself. We had done it. We were in Wales. We had done more than just move country; we had turned our lives around and shifted to a different mode of being. It was wonderful to lie there and hear only the birds; no traffic, no neighbours. Through a chink in the curtains I could glimpse green as the branches of the ancient holly tree outside the cottage swayed gently in the breeze.

After a hasty breakfast, we finished unpacking the Jeep and made an inventory of immediate necessities. It was Christmas Eve, so it wasn't the day to do any major shopping. But we needed to buy food, coal, and candles. We also needed some spare gas mantles. We had managed to work out how to light the gas lights: you had to hold a lit match under the mantle and wait for it to catch. When it did, the flame would race up the mantle at an alarming speed, but then would (hopefully) settle down to a soft yellow glow. The mantles, we discovered, were quite fragile; we broke one almost immediately by touching the body of the mantle rather than holding it by the little plastic base.

We made our way into Llanrwst, proceeding slowly down the track. The night before, unused to the terrain and anxious to get to the cottage as quickly as possible, we had driven a little too fast over the rocky parts of the track. The result had been a bone-shaking journey that left us both a bit shocked and wondering whether the track was too much even for the Jeep. But in daylight, and at a slower pace, it was less daunting. We realized that one had to ease the Jeep over the rocky parts, tensing one's body against the impact. You could go a little faster over the areas that were less rocky because these were filled with mud and so made a softer surface.

The little town was pretty with Christmas lights and had a festive bustle. We were pleased to find a well-stocked fruit and veg store and an interesting whole foods shop. We managed to find most of what we needed. However, Llanrwst had no hardware store and our enquiries about gas mantles in the Spar met with uncomprehending looks from the teenage shop assistant. We settled for a cheap bottle of champagne and a mini Christmas cake and raced back to the hill before the weather turned.

For Christmas lunch, we had vegetables cooked on the camping stove and potatoes cooked in the fire. After lunch, we wandered across the hillside, jumping the little stream by the alder trees, lightheaded on champagne, cold mountain air, and the thrill of adventure. It was cold with a light frost, and not much warmer in the cottage. We took a couple of baskets with us to collect fallen twigs for kindling.

But first, we went to inspect our water source. This was a natural spring that bubbled from a peat bog. We had discovered that the name of the house was Tyn-y-Bryn, which means smallholding by the stream. This perfectly described the hillside around the cottage, which was alive with little streams crisscrossing the landscape. Before buying the cottage, we had arranged to have the water quality checked. The man from the water board who came to take samples had looked doubtfully at the spring and told us that it was highly unlikely that the water would be fit for consumption. However, the report he eventually sent us declared the water to be 'of excellent quality.' The spring had passed with flying colours.

To make access to the water easier, a plastic box had been constructed around the spring to act as a reservoir, and had been fenced off against the surrounding sheep and cows. However, over the summer the cows had trampled the ground outside the fence, allowing muddy water to seep into the spring enclosure. Channels would have to be excavated and the spring box thoroughly cleaned before we could use the water. That meant we had no clean drinking water. We cursed ourselves for not buying bottled water from Llanrwst.

As we headed back to the cottage with our baskets of twiggery, we reflected on a curious thing. In the city, when contemplating the move, we had been anxious about the deprivations we were going to face. How were we going to cope with minimal heating, no bathroom, and no electricity? Now we were here, those concerns seemed foolish. The night before, we had cooked on an open fire and washed in the kitchen sink. But it hadn't seemed like an inconvenience. It hadn't dented our happiness one bit; it was part of the adventure. We had no modern conveniences now but we had other things instead: a beautiful hillside, an immense sky, and peace. It seemed like a fair exchange.

7

Those first weeks back at work after Christmas were a heady mix of excitement and hard labour. Because of the lengthy commute and the time it took to get the Jeep down the track and through several gates, we had to get up ridiculously early. It was usually me who forced myself out of bed first and went downstairs to put the kettle on for warm water to wash with. The cottage was freezing in the mornings and our strip washes at the sink had to be carried out fast (and usually with gritted teeth). It wasn't worth lighting the fire for the half hour it took to wash and pack the Jeep. The latter task was usually Geoff's responsibility, and involved several trips down the track to the Jeep, which was parked about a hundred metres from the house. Many mornings, these trips were done in torchlight and driving rain.

One morning we almost got the Jeep stuck. To speed things up in the morning, we had parked right in front of the cottage the evening before. However, it rained heavily overnight, turning the track to thick mud. When we tried to drive up the slope in the morning, the wheels spun wildly and Buffy started sliding further back down the slope towards the stream. We eventually managed to get out by shovelling bits of stone and gravel in front of the wheels to gain some purchase. From then on, we only parked by the house in very dry weather when there was no forecast of rain.

We decided early on that the Jeep was female. Her registration number contained the letters B, F, and Y so we named her Buffy. Previous cars we had owned had been useful but unremarkable means of getting from A to B. Buffy was different. She was an essential part of the whole adventure. Selling our city car to buy an off-road vehicle like Buffy signified for us a shift from the safety of urban normalcy to the thrill of life in the wilds. We often received curious glances when parking in the university car park after our morning journey. Unless the weather had been fine, Buffy would be filthy after splashing down the track and her big tyres would be caked with mud. Like Buffy, we too would arrive at work somewhat dishevelled.

After trekking down the track to Buffy, and (in Geoff's case) having to get out of the car to open several gates, we were usually soaked by the time we started the drive to work. Thankfully, Buffy had a powerful heater so we sat and steamed during the drive, drying out slowly.

To cope with the elements we had both taken to wearing outdoor clothes, as they were hard-wearing, quick drying, and didn't need ironing. Abandoning our smart city clothes to wear technical tee-shirts, fleeces, and walking boots felt liberating. It was like putting on a different skin, one that more accurately reflected our lives on the hill. A year ago, I would have been horrified to wear a jacket that smelt of mountain air and woodsmoke, and boots with mud clinging to them. Now, I relished these signs of our return to a more natural environment.

Travelling back to the city, going through the routine of the working day, we sometimes felt like conspirators, like we had a secret no-one else knew. Although people at work knew we had moved to an isolated cottage in the country, most were unaware of the true extent of our privation. It was fun to sometimes shock them with the occasional description of conditions we were starting to take for granted. I remember greeting a colleague one cold winter morning as she came hurrying down the corridor swathed in heavy coat and woolly hat and gloves.

'It's freezing out there!' she complained.

As I nodded agreement, something occurred to her. 'Ooh, I bet it's cold in your little cottage isn't it?'

'It certainly is,' I replied. 'There was ice on the inside of our bedroom window this morning!'

'You're joking!' she said.

'In fact,' I said, 'there was also ice in my hair!'

'Oh good God!' she exclaimed, a look of true horror on her face. 'I really couldn't live like that!' She regarded me curiously. 'Don't you regret it sometimes? You know, living without central heating and other things?'

I shook my head firmly. 'No I don't.'

Later, I reflected whether I would have given her a different answer had she asked me earlier that same morning, as I made my way downstairs by torchlight to a freezing kitchen. Then I remembered our short walk down the track to Buffy. A few stars had still been out, glinting through the bare branches of the sycamores. The cold air had smelt pure and sweet. We had both been quiet that morning, tired and grumpy because of the cold.

Geoff had suddenly grabbed my arm and hissed 'Look!'

In the pale pre-dawn light, a huge white shape glided silently past us and down the hill to the old barn near the stream.

'What on earth was that?'

'I'm not sure but I think it was a barn owl. It must be living in that old building. I've never seen one before.'

Neither had I. And now it seemed we were living next door to one. The rare sighting was like a gift, waking us up to the beauty of the hill and how lucky we were to be living there. If we had to give up central heating and other home comforts for that, it was a price worth paying. At work that day, I carried around with me the memory of the owl, and it gave me a warm glow.

Although exhilarating, those first few weeks after our move were a steep learning curve. Neither of us had lived 'off-system' before. When you have lived your whole life with the conveniences of hot and cold running water, electricity at the flick of a switch, and modern sanitation, living without them takes some getting used to. Essentially, we had travelled back a couple of hundred years overnight. With no urban light pollution, the night skies on the hill were spectacular. I had never seen so many stars. On clear nights the Milky Way was easily visible. There were no street lights on the hill, so we learnt to cherish the full moon, which lit our way when we were coming home on dark winter nights.

Lighting the inside of the cottage was more tricky. Firelight and candlelight were wonderful to relax to in the evenings. However, it was difficult to cook, read, or generally move about the house by candlelight. We discovered that climbing the stairs to bed while balancing a candle in a candlestick, although romantic, was harder than it looked in old black and white films. In our draughty cottage, the candle was liable to blow out at the most inconvenient moment. And carrying the candleholder in one hand while cupping the other hand around the flickering flame to stop it blowing out meant that one couldn't carry anything else. We rarely lit the gas lamps as we still hadn't found a source of spare gas mantles. Instead, we used small LED head torches for navigation and any activities that needed better illumination. In winter, this meant that we wore the torches most of the time. In fact, the two most important items in my less than glamorous wardrobe during our time on the hill were a head torch and wellington boots.

Drinking water was also a problem. We had been waiting for a dryish day to clean out the spring box and repair the fence, but it seemed to rain every weekend. In the meantime, we had been buying large bottles of mineral water and carrying them from Buffy to the house. We needed an easier (and cheaper) solution. For washing, we had been using rainwater from a huge wooden water butt that was fed by a downpipe on the front wall of the cottage. This water looked reasonably clear, as long as you didn't look too closely. We decided to take a chance and use it for drinking water too. However, we took the precaution of boiling it first. It would be inconvenient to drop dead before we had finished the renovation.

Another thing we had to adapt to was living something of a double life. We envied the Wests, who after saving up to buy their 'hovel in the hills', resigned from their jobs and left the city for good. Until we had paid off our loan for the cottage and finished renovating it, we couldn't give up work. For the moment, we had to settle for living the rural dream during the evenings and weekends. And we had to be careful to maintain the right professional image at work. One or two of our colleagues were openly disapproving of our escape, and seemed to believe that we had moved to Wales purely make it easier to slope off work. We sensed that they were waiting for an opportunity to confirm their suspicions and were determined to prove them wrong.

Despite the long commute, we usually managed to arrive at work very early and always in time to effect a quick change of image. Walking boots were exchanged for tidy shoes, and tee-shirts swapped for shirts. We both kept a set of formal ironed clothes in the office for occasions like graduation. I spent a few minutes in the bathroom after arriving at work tying back my dishevelled hair into something approximating respectability.

But conditions were still primitive at the cottage. Geoff cooked our evening meal on the one ring of the camping stove, but it was time-consuming and laboursome. To speed things up in the morning, we would grab a hasty cooked breakfast at a motorway service station on the way to work. We felt like nomads; nearly always on the road, constantly packing and unpacking. Buffy was always full with bags of books and marking, laundry, gas bottles, coal, and logs.

Although we had pared down our wardrobes, laundry was always a problem. Several kettle-loads of water were needed to wash and rinse a few clothes, and by the time the whole process had been completed the weather had usually turned and it was too wet to hang anything out to dry. At eight hundred metres above sea level, the microclimate on our hill could produce horizontal rain, wind, blazing sunshine, and freezing cold mists, sometimes within the same day. We learnt early on that it was pointless to hastily wash a few clothes and hang them out before racing off to work. Some days, we left to a clear sky and strong sunlight only to return to pelting rain and washing that was a lot wetter than when it had been pegged out.

So after some enquiries, we found an excellent laundry service in Llanrwst. Each week, we dropped a bag of laundry off at Glynis' on our way to work and collected it, washed, dried, and beautifully folded, on Saturday mornings. Friendly and shrewd, Glynis dispensed advice and kept us up to date on all the latest local news and gossip. Sometimes, if Glynis was on holiday or if we were particularly pressed for time, we would do our laundry at my parents', who lived not far from the university. We were finding that some aspects of living 'the simple life' were a lot more complicated than we had expected.

Our family and friends were keen to come and see the cottage but we managed to delay them until we had established a basic level of order. Thankfully, the absence of a bathroom put most visitors off staying overnight. We had cleaned out the main bedroom and assembled the bed but we still had no wardrobe, so the room was half full of bags of clothes. With the mattress gone from the sitting room, we were able to assemble the sofa. This, together with an old leather chair, was the only seating. We had brought an old pine dining table with us but we had no dining chairs as we hadn't been able to fit them in Buffy. Nevertheless, our first visitors arrived with the spring, and the warmer weather.

I was sure my parents would hate the place. When we had shown my father the estate agent's details of the house, he had been so worried about the lack of facilities and the access he had tried to talk us out of buying it. Yet when we walked up the little rise and he got his first view of the cottage and distant mountains he shook his head in wonder.

'Well,' he said, 'Now I can see why you're doing this.'

We took my parents to the edge of the hillside to see the magnificent view. The land sloped more steeply here and carried the gaze down to the valley, thick with trees. The mountains rose up sharply, filling the horizon. I turned to see my mother sobbing quietly.

'Mum! What's wrong?'

'Nothing,' she mumbled. 'It's just ... it's just that I've never seen anywhere so beautiful.'

We discovered that, like us, most visitors were so smitten by the house and its setting that its deficiencies seemed of little importance. A work colleague who came up waxed lyrical about the hillside and the garden but when he ducked his head under the door lintel into the sitting room, he laughed out loud. I was surprised and a little disappointed at his laughter. But then he looked around the room and beamed.

'It's like a cave,' he exclaimed. 'It's so dark!'

He touched the rough stone walls and looked at the huge oak beams. His gaze took in the six or seven candles, which did little to penetrate the gloom on that cloudy day.

'It's a bit rough and ready,' I said apologetically. 'There's a lot of work to do still …'

'No, no,' he interrupted me. 'It's perfect. It's an outrageous place to live, but it's perfect. How much do you want for it?'

8

Psychologists and psychoanalysts have long considered the house to be a metaphor of the self. The dwellings of our dreams and imagination reflect something of who we are and who we wish to be. In myths, fairytales, and literature, houses shelter and conceal us from the world, but can also imprison us. Think of the romance of Sleeping Beauty's castle, slumbering behind an impenetrable thicket of briar roses, the menace of Grandma's cottage in the woods in *Little Red Riding Hood*, and the warm safety of Bilbo Baggins' cozy hobbit house.

But our houses are not just practical shelters from the elements. The places we inhabit, whether they are mansions, bedsits, or caves, feed our souls. 'Soul' in this sense is what the Jungian psychologist James Hillman has defined as the 'imaginative possibility in our natures.' Our dwellings, where we are housed, change us as much as we change them. Whether it is our memories of a long-lost beloved childhood home or our longing for some ideal future home that is perfect in every way, houses furnish the psyche with rich images and ideas. In *The Poetics of Space*, his fascinating study of how we experience the spaces we call home, the philosopher Gaston Bachelard considers how the elements of a house, its attics and cellars, windowseats and wardrobes, fuel the imagination and inspire our creativity.

In modern times, we search for myths and meanings of the house in television programmes like *Grand Designs* and *Escape to the Country*. There is something compelling about vicariously watching other people search for their dream homes. We appraise each house in terms of our own desires and dreams, imagining ourselves inhabiting that particular cottage or this particular converted barn. And how often does the house hunter value the 'feel' of a particular place over its size or other characteristics? What we are searching for is not merely the house itself but a certain quality of inhabiting or being in a house. It is how we experience a house that is important.

In the city, we often felt constrained in our house. We came to realize that this was not because the house was too small for us and our belongings, but because it provided an insufficient retreat from the outside world. The stout walls failed to shut out the noise of cars and close neighbours. The exhaust fumes from the heavy traffic drifted in through the gaps in the old window frames. The boundary between inside and outside seemed to become more permeable with time.

In modern times, we often have huge expectations about our homes. I remember my Gran's kitchen in the 1970s, which contained a meat safe and a tiny larder where she kept her butter and cheese. When my parents finally persuaded her to buy a refrigerator, she hardly used it. She treated the shiny new white addition with suspicion bordering on resentment and continued to keep most of her food in the larder. Just off the kitchen was a small scullery which was home to an old top-loading washing machine and a mangle. Gran flatly refused to exchange her mangle for a new-fangled spin dryer, insisting on spending hours in the freezing cold scullery every Monday doing her laundry the 'proper' way.

My Gran would be astonished at the modern wish lists of many house hunters: huge kitchen-diners with bespoke larders, multiple ensuite bathrooms, and walk-in wardrobes. Today, many people want family homes big enough to allow each child their own bedroom. After we had been living in the cottage for a few years, we made the acquaintance of Gwyn, an elderly gentleman who was born in the cottage and had grown up in the 1920s and 1930s. He told us many fascinating stories about life on the hillside. Gwyn was from a large family and had five siblings. He described how four of the six children had shared the largest of the cottage bedrooms, which is small by modern standards. A curtain was hung down the middle of the room to provide separate sleeping spaces for the three boys and three girls. Similarly, a curtain provided two sleeping spaces in the smaller bedroom, which is open to the stairs, and which slept Gwyn's parents and the two youngest children.

Perhaps we seek more spacious houses as a kind of compensation for our crowded cities and lack of access to large outdoor spaces. Although the cottage was much smaller than the city house we had left, we felt less constrained. With a large garden and several acres of wild hillside to explore, it suddenly seemed unimportant that we were living in a house that had about the same space and rather fewer facilities than the average caravan.

The kitchen was the smallest room and was a galley space, long and narrow. On one side was the sink and camping stove, which stood on a shelf of thick Welsh slate. Underneath the shelf was a small water tank. This had to be filled by hand through a hole in the top. The shelf continued along the wall to the sink. On the opposite wall were two old kitchen units that, although in a dubious avocado green colour, were in reasonable condition.

At one end of the kitchen was a door to our walk-in larder. Do not get excited at this point. The 'larder' was a cramped space under the stairs that was full of spiders. We gained access to this space by cutting a hole in the thin boards that separated the kitchen from the stairs. Geoff made a latched wooden door to fit the gap, turning the space into a small but serviceable cupboard. Once we had cleaned out and painted the cupboard and put up two shelves, it made a perfect little larder. We had heard, but not seen, mice in there but they seemed to disappear after our cat Bunna, who was a fearsome little hunter, had patrolled the cupboard once or twice. As that part of the kitchen was half underground, the cupboard was always cool. We kept our dairy goods on a marble chopping board on one of the shelves. The previous owner had left behind a calor gas-powered fridge. However, this never seemed to work properly and took up precious space in the kitchen. We soon abandoned it and just used the larder.

We discovered that there was a reason for the cold slate shelves in the kitchen. Gwyn told us that when he lived there, what we called the sitting room was in fact the kitchen. His mother, Eleanor, cooked the family's meals on a small range set into the inglenook. In Gwyn's day, our kitchen was Eleanor's dairy and larder. The large hooks we had noticed set into the beams were apparently for hanging hams. Gwyn showed us where a piece of wood had been cut out of one of the low beams in the ceiling. He explained that this was where a wheel had been fixed for churning butter. Eleanor made butter for the family but also enough to sell. Each week, she would walk the several miles to the market at Llanrwst to sell her butter.

Eleanor's mother, Manon (Gwyn's grandmother), lived in a cottage not far away but further up the hillside. One day, we went searching for Manon's cottage. After scrambling around on the hillside for an hour or two we found the little dwelling and ducked in through the low doorway. There was just one tiny window, which let in very little light on that overcast day. In the gloom, we could just make out the remains of Manon's fireplace and a few slate flagstones. We were shocked by how small her house was; it was little more than one room with what looked like an attached animal pen. Whereas our cottage was in a sheltered position and surrounded by trees, Manon's cottage was on an exposed stretch of hillside. In its state of half-dereliction, under a lowering sky, it had a melancholy air. It must have been a harsh existence for Manon, especially in winter. Cottages high in the hills were not designed to be lived in all year round. They were 'hafods': summer houses for the shepherds who tended the sheep on these highland pastures. However, many families, like Gwyn's, lived in them all year round because they could not afford to rent a house in the valley.

The recent social and economic changes caused by the COVID-19 pandemic have precipitated a modern housing crisis. As we move into a global recession, it is harder to get on the property ladder or to cover spiralling rental costs. Many people are also questioning the desirability of acquiring almost lifelong debt in order to obtain a dream home. A large expensive house, no matter how luxurious, may seem like a gilded cage if one cannot pay the mortgage. It is perhaps not surprising that there is a growing interest in so-called 'tiny houses'. These range from small, affordable purpose-built dwellings to more imaginative house solutions such as converted vans, trailers, and narrowboats. There seems to be a growing awareness that quality of life is more important than money and lots of possessions, and that the latter do not necessarily guarantee the former.

Living on the hillside, our priorities began to change. We quickly realized that life in the city had not really prepared us for the hardships of living off-system. The exhilaration of our new life was shot through with many stressful moments. We had taken for granted the convenience of flicking a switch to flood a room with light, or running a hot bath to wash off the dirt and sweat after a day labouring in the garden. We were surprised how long simple jobs took when they had to be done by torchlight, how much longer it took to get warm when one had to build, light, and feed a fire rather than switch on a heater. In those early weeks, we found ourselves occasionally bickering when the tiredness caught up with us or when a repair job at the cottage had gone wrong.

We also struggled with money. The repayments on the loan for the cottage were higher than our previous mortgage. In addition, we had monthly payments for Buffy, who ate petrol at an alarming rate. And although we didn't need to buy any furniture, there always seemed to be unexpected but essential purchases: new wellington boots, a wheelbarrow, waterproof trousers, fencing to keep the sheep out of the garden, a new axe.

However, as that first cold winter eased into spring, we found ourselves adapting to our pre-modern living arrangements. The pitch darkness of a moonless night soon began to seem comforting rather than unnerving. Instead of fretting about not having enough light to read by in the evenings, we blew out the candles and sat and talked by firelight. We began to appreciate the pleasure in simple physical chores like chopping wood and going down to the spring to collect water.

Engaging in these manual tasks provided a sense of

reconnection, an energy that we hadn't felt in the city, cocooned against the natural world in our comfortable house. Although modern technologies such as washing machines, television, and central heating make life much easier, they come at the cost of a disconnection from some of the physical realities of life. After a week spent in overheated lecture halls and meeting rooms, or in the office in front of a computer screen, it was often a relief to spend weekends immersed in physical tasks such as constructing garden beds or rebuilding the porch. We felt more embodied, more real.

This greater connection with place was reflected in the ways in which we became integrated into our new community. Unlike anywhere else we had lived before, our new house had a name, not a number. The name of the house expressed certain characteristics of the hillside, rooting it firmly in the landscape. We too felt rooted. We liked the way that our identities became merged with that of the house; our neighbours often referred to each other by their house names, not their personal names. This, we were sure, was partly because almost everyone in the area was either a Roberts, a Jones, or a Williams. A comment to your neighbour about Mr Roberts' new sheepdog, for example, could quickly become confusing unless your neighbour knew to which of the eight Mr Roberts in the village you were referring. The problem was solved by referring to Mr Roberts' house, Tyn-y-Bont, (which means 'house by the bridge') rather than the man himself, as in 'I hear that Tyn-y-Bont has got a new sheepdog.' Like Welsh place names, the names of dwellings are not arbitrary but express the way the house is situated in the landscape. If you knew the name of a person's house, you had a good idea where in the locale you could find it. We loved being known as 'Tyn-y-Bryn' rather than 'the Wynnes'.

Unlike in the city, the village community was close-knit. In this rural area, neighbours looked out for each other and supported one another. And news, such as an English couple moving into the cottage on the hill, travelled fast. Only a few weeks after moving in, one of our friends decided to make a surprise visit. She found our village but had no idea how to get to the house from there. Neither could she remember the name of the house. She stopped the car and asked the first villager she saw, an elderly man who she found leaning on his front gate contemplating the world. We often saw this man when we drove through the village. We had exchanged friendly waves but had never spoken to him. Our friend took a chance and told him simply that she was looking for the couple who had just bought the cottage on the hill.

'Oh, you'll be wanting Tyn-y-Bryn,' he said.

'Will I?'

'Oh yes ... but it's not easy to get to the house, you know. You'll never make it in that,' he said, regarding her rust bucket of an old car.

He gave her detailed directions of which track to take and where she should leave the car and walk.

'I hope they're in after all this!' she said.

'Oh, you'll find them in alright,' he assured her. 'I saw them drive back from town half an hour ago. They're probably in for the day now; it's not often they drive out on Sunday afternoons!'

After recovering from her uphill trek, she told us about the encounter. With a worried frown, she said, 'I think you should be careful, you know. That old man looks harmless enough, but he seems very well-informed about your habits. Are you sure he's not ex-CIA?'

9

In tackling the everyday problems of life at the cottage, we sometimes felt we were in one of those historical reality television documentaries, in which ordinary people have to spend several weeks as if they are living in the 1940s or the Stone Age. It sometimes felt that, with our low-tech lifestyle, we had gone back a hundred years. However, we had no historical experts to advise us or provide the resources we needed to live off the system.

We had at least managed to sort out the spring. Geoff cleaned out the spring box, removing two frogs who had decided to set up home in there. He also dug channels around the perimeter of the enclosure fence so that dirty water from outside the enclosure would be channelled away from the spring box. We now had plenty of pure clean spring water to drink, with one snag. The spring was situated a hundred or so metres downhill from the cottage, so all water had to be laboriously carried uphill. On a warm sunny day this was quite a pleasant task. In driving rain or snow it was rather more trying. Several parts of the path down to the spring were tricky. You had to watch your footing when crossing the little stream and it was easy to twist an ankle on the uneven ground near the old barn.

Even on the way down, with empty 10-litre water carriers, the trip provided a workout. Coming back up, it could be heavy going. If we were at the cottage all day we usually had to make two trips to the spring, one in the morning and one in the evening. We still had to boil the kettle to obtain hot water but at least now we didn't have to boil our drinking water too. We knew that the spring water was pure, but we used a heavy-duty water filter as an extra precaution.

With no bathroom and no hot running water, we had to adapt to more old-fashioned bathing techniques. In a local antique shop we found a nicely painted Victorian porcelain jug and bowl, the type that would have stood on a bedroom wash stand. However, the frigid temperature of our bedroom made it an uninviting place to take a wash. Instead, we took to washing in front of the sitting room fire, which was rather more cozy. The bowl would be set on a towel in front of the fire and the jug used to carry warm water in from the kitchen. One drawback with this system was that the jug and bowl, which were both sturdy pieces, were uncomfortably heavy when filled with water. We were soon hunting for alternatives.

We struck lucky one day in the antique shop-cum-cafe we had found on our first visit to Llanrwst. We bought two old enamel wash bowls which were much lighter than the porcelain. One was a simple bowl with a painted orange rim. The other bowl was oval with a small recess for soap and a hook for hanging it up. We used these two wash bowls for many years; they lived on a shelf in the porch.

We grew to love bathing in front of a crackling fire. We were so far off the beaten track that we usually didn't bother to close the curtains when bathing. We just kept an eye out in case the farmer who owned the pasture land surrounding the cottage should drive past on his quad bike or in case a stray hill walker knocked to ask directions.

One afternoon, not long after moving in, our neighbour Beti, who lived down the hill, strolled up to say hello. I was having a fireside wash but of course had not bothered to close the curtains. Hearing voices, I peeked out carefully to see Beti about to walk up the front path from where she would almost certainly see me. Luckily, Geoff was working in the garden and spotted her as she reached the front gate. He engaged her in conversation, but of course was unable to invite her in for a cup of tea. Eventually, she left to walk back home, no doubt wondering at our lack of neighbourly hospitality! Once we got to know Beti better, we realized that we hadn't needed to feel embarrassed. She would have roared with kindly laughter if she had known the real reason the house was off limits that day.

We spent a lot of time in the early days hunting for simple practical objects that were of good quality. We quickly realized that many of the simple household objects that our grandparents would have taken for granted were very hard to source and often poorly made. More and more, products seem to be made to satisfy the eye with little regard for whether they fulfil the purpose they were intended for. For example, it was a constant struggle to find good quality candles. In an era where one could buy electric cars, flatscreen televisions, and ever more powerful personal computers, it was impossible, it seemed, to find a teapot that poured properly or candles that functioned for more than a night or two. We became candle connoisseurs, and at the slightest encouragement could give long and boring descriptions of the qualities of the perfect candle. For instance, we found that many candles that looked well-made had inferior wicks that ceased to burn properly after a short time, resulting in the whole candle having to be thrown away. Others had good wicks but poor quality wax, so that the candle gradually melted into a sticky mess. It was my parents who chanced on some large good quality church candles in their local supermarket. Every time they went shopping they bought us a few more candles. They were welcome gifts and kept our sitting room lit for months, until the supermarket stopped stocking them.

We eventually managed to track down some gas mantles. A neighbour told us about an 'old-fashioned' hardware store in Menai Bridge, on Anglesey, and we set out one Saturday to find it. It is a picturesque drive over the Menai Strait to the island of Anglesey. We found Menai Bridge to be a small attractive town overlooking the Strait and well stocked with interesting shops and cafes.

On the short high street we were thrilled to find the largest hardware shop we had ever seen. It may sound strange, but after months scouring the area for necessities, the sight of this huge treasure house of 'real' objects was thrilling. The shop was in an old three-storey Victorian building. The large bay windows on the ground floor displayed every type of utility ware, from enamel cooking pots to axes. The contents of the shop spilled onto the pavement, which showcased a wonderful collection of wooden-handled brooms, metal buckets, and wicker baskets. Inside the shop, old wooden and glass counters were filled with boxes of smaller items like nuts, bolts, and screws. Behind the counters, floor to ceiling shelves were crammed with what must have been thousands of boxes of esoteric hardware items. We hoped that somewhere in this pleasing disorder lay some gas mantles.

We seemed to be in luck. Upon our enquiry, a large jovial man in a brown overall gave us an affirmative nod rather than a look of incomprehension. He fetched a ladder and climbed to one of the dizzyingly high shelves to rummage around. Eventually, he brought down three boxes.

'Which size mantle do you want?' he asked.

It hadn't occurred to us that there was more than one size. We hadn't even known what a gas mantle looked like before moving to Tyn-y-Bryn. We hedged our bets and bought one of each size, surprised at how expensive they were. At that price, we wouldn't be able to use the gas lights for long periods. We must have spent a couple of hours in that wonderful shop, emerging with not just the gas mantles but with many other items we had spent months looking for. I was particularly happy with a box of Granny's Soap Flakes. I had been searching without success for a simple pure soap product for the occasional handwashing of clothes. Our kitchen water drained into a sump that ran under the kitchen garden, but unless it was raining we tended to empty our modest washing water directly onto the flowerbeds in the front garden. We therefore used cleaning products that were as free from artificial chemicals as possible. The soap flakes would be a more natural laundry detergent.

We loaded up Buffy and then looked for a cafe. At the end of the high street was an interesting-looking eaterie with mismatched wooden tables and chairs and terracotta pots of flowers and herbs arranged outside. We celebrated our modest hardware haul with an excellent vegetarian breakfast and a large pot of Earl Grey tea. We made a mental note to pay a return visit to Menai Bridge.

Before we left, we wandered round the antique shops. Looking in the window of one little shop, I grabbed Geoff's arm.

'Look! A chamber pot! And it looks intact.'

The chamber pot was another item on our permanent wish list of elusive traditional household items. Where does one buy a chamber pot on a modern high street? We had taken to trawling all the antique and second-hand shops we came across as these were often the only places that stocked the essentials we needed for our pre-modern lifestyle. Most antique shops sold chamber pots, but often they were cracked or otherwise unsuitable for real use.

Although we had no bathroom, we did have a toilet. However, in true peasant style, our toilet was outside. Next to the cottage was a small wooden structure encircled by a wall. This was Ty Bach (literally the 'little house' in Welsh). Ty Bach housed our portable toilet and, we hoped, was a temporary solution until we constructed a proper compost toilet. Beneath the toilet bowl of the portable loo was a detachable chamber to collect the waste, which was sprinkled with sawdust after each use. We had managed to find an area of deeper soil in our stony garden and had, with great difficulty, dug a hole. The contents of the toilet were emptied into this hole, along with kitchen waste and cardboard and then covered up. We planned to then fill the hole in with soil and plant fruit trees over it. It wasn't ideal, but it was the best we could manage.

We had to be careful though, in tending to our compost pits. One day, caught short while tearing up cardboard to add to the heap, Geoff decided that it was easier to add just a little more urine to the compost rather than racing to Ty Bach. After looking over at the track to check there were no walkers about, he stood liberally 'watering' the compost and gazing at the hillside just beyond the track. To his horror, he caught sight of a seated figure. It was Sian, a neighbour from one of the farms just down the hill. Mortified, Geoff tried to shuffle out of view, hoping that Sian was gazing at the mountains rather than at our garden! When we next met her, Sian gave nothing away, so we could only wonder exactly what she was looking at that particular afternoon. Needless to say, Geoff's future fertilization efforts were preceded by an almost obsessive examination of the surrounding vantage points.

Our plans for the cottage included some building

work. Adjacent to the house was a tumbledown structure containing the remains of an old fireplace. This may have been an older cottage or perhaps an adjacent bakehouse or other outbuilding that the occupants had ceased to use. We planned to rebuild this structure and then knock through into it from our existing sitting room. The footprint of the ruined building wasn't large but it would be sufficient to allow for a good-sized kitchen and a separate compost loo and bathroom, with perhaps a mezzanine floor for a sleeping loft. However, the project would take years. We would have to tackle it ourselves, because even if we had been able to afford to pay them, the cottage's remoteness and difficult access would put off any sensible builder.

In the meantime, we had to make do with Ty Bach. We quickly became used to our 'loo with a view' and even became hardened to the discomfort of having to trudge through snow and rain to use it. However, visiting our outdoor loo on winter nights was a trying experience. On cold wet nights, I would lie there as long as I could, trying to ignore the urge to visit Ty Bach. Eventually, grumbling as quietly as I could so as not to wake Geoff, I would haul myself out of the warm bed and throw on some clothes as fast as possible. If it was wet or snowy I would also have to pull on wellies and a waterproof before creeping quietly outside. Usually, I would be accosted by one of our cats, who would decide to follow me to the toilet in case my pockets were miraculously stuffed with cat biscuits. By the time I had hurried back inside (dodging the cats), undressed, and crawled back into bed, I was freezing and thoroughly awake. It was a lot of work to spend a penny, hence the need for a chamber pot, which at least would provide a simpler means of relief at night.

The chamber pot we bought in Menai Bridge was perfect and made night-time visits to Ty Bach a thing of the past. However, while cleaning the pot out one morning, I managed to crack it. It was a good excuse for another pilgrimage to Menai Bridge, and another good breakfast at the pretty cafe we liked. After picking up some gas mantles at the hardware store, we revisited the antique shop where we had found the first pot. Luckily, we found another chamber pot in good condition which to my delight was a little bigger than the first one. What luxury! The shop owner remembered us and seemed a little surprised at our purchase of another chamber pot.

'Are you painting them?' he asked.

'No,' I said.

'Oh. Some people put flowers in them,' he tried.

'Yes,' I said, hoping he would assume I was doing the same.

For a moment, I was tempted to tell him about Ty Bach, about the fact that for us an antique chamber pot was a necessity not an ornament. But I resisted. I wasn't embarrassed about our way of life, but I suspected he might be. So I merely smiled enigmatically and hurried away gratefully with my precious pot.

10

Despite the work that needed doing to the house, we knew we needed to get the garden into some sort of shape if we were to be self-sufficient in food. We were due to give up our allotment in Liverpool at the end of the season, but we were still harvesting sweetcorn, tomatoes, and lots of other vegetables from our small plot. We had applied for and obtained an allotment in Wales, at a picturesque site near Conwy. The allotments were fringed by mature trees and had a view of the sea. Most evenings after work we spent an hour tending our Liverpool allotment before driving back to Wales. Sunday afternoons we spent on the Conwy allotment and the rest of the weekend was spent working in the garden.

And it needed a lot of work. Like the rest of the hillside, the garden consisted of scrubland and rocks. Only a shallow layer of acidic soil covered the rock. There were several small stone outcrops, which meant that most of the plantable areas sloped, but in different directions. The lowest part of the garden was damp because it gave on to a small boggy meadow, which Gwyn told us was called Cae Bach ('small field'). When we moved in, we had to share the garden with the sheep owned by our neighbour Tomos.

There was a rough fence marking the boundary between Tomos' land and our garden, but this was in some disrepair. And Tomos' sheep were excellent jumpers.

Driving to Llanrwst one day, we came upon Tomos' Land Rover parked askew in the lane. In the winter, he kept some of his sheep in the field next to this particular lane. But that day, a good number of them were in the lane, Tomos in their midst. A trampled gap in the hedgerow revealed their escape route.

'We should get out and help him,' Geoff said.

'Wait,' I said. 'Look.'

Tomos had made his way back to the Land Rover and was opening the door. A black and white bundle of energy leapt out and we recognized Gwilym, his favourite sheepdog. At a curt command from Tomos, Gwilym raced down the lane to head off the escape party. Tomos stood by the Land Rover issuing the occasional command. It was a joy to watch the dog darting purposefully around the small flock. Within a few minutes, Gwilym had rounded up the strays and ushered them back through the gap in the hedge. Tomos moved the Land Rover to let us pass and we paused to have a few words with him.

We liked Tomos. Taciturn and rather shy, he was a kind-natured man with calm blue eyes and a face that reflected almost eighty years of Snowdonia weather. Conversations with Tomos could be time-consuming, as he thought carefully before each utterance and spoke slowly. His unhurried ways seemed to speak of an earlier era and were in contrast to our own busy lifestyle. When we spoke of driving to the city each day, his eyes would widen in disbelief. We suspected that he rarely left the village. He seemed thoroughly happy with his sheep and his land.

Tomos told us that the landlord of the pub had phoned to tell him that the sheep were loose.

'They'll always break out if they can,' he observed.

He gazed at the sheep, now grazing peacefully. 'I like my sheep,' he said contentedly.

'Your sheep are very athletic,' Geoff said with a grin. 'Just when we think we've made the fence high enough, one will manage to vault over it when we're not looking!'

'Oh yes,' Tomos said proudly. 'They're champion jumpers, my sheep!'

Fencing the garden off from the animals was a priority if we were to grow any food. We invested in several rolls of the sturdiest chicken wire, bought from the local agricultural suppliers. We acquired some hardwood fence posts from a friend of ours who was a tree surgeon. Once the fence was complete, we were able to start growing food. However, constant vigilance was needed to check the fence for any weak points, particularly any areas that seemed to be sagging, and therefore jumpable. Tomos' sheep would stand outside the fence gazing in covetously at our fruit and vegetables. If a sheep got in while we were at work, we knew that it could decimate our crops in a very short space of time.

The cattle were less of a problem, but they could get into different kinds of trouble. One day, we were working in the garden round the back of the house when we heard a tremendous clanging noise that seemed to be coming from the front garden. We raced round to find Tomos' new little bull in a frantic state. The front gate, which was a little loose, had swung open and the youngster had trotted in to explore. He had decided to investigate our wheelbarrow, which was a large steel one. Unfortunately, he had got his small horns caught in the handlebars and was proceeding to stagger round the garden firmly attached to the wheelbarrow. The poor creature was obviously terrified, and was shaking his head frantically from side to side, banging the wheelbarrow against the picnic table. We knew we had to try and free him before he did himself some serious damage.

We approached slowly; I positioned myself to block the bull's access to the back garden and Geoff blocked his access to the open front gate. The bull stopped and stood there uncertainly, breathing heavily. Geoff moved forward quickly and, quite literally, took the bull by the horns and tried to disentangle the wheelbarrow. The bull backed away in alarm but his route was blocked by Sylvie, the large sycamore tree at the front of the cottage. Geoff made a second attempt and managed this time to hold on to the bull, who put up little resistance. The animal was probably exhausted at that point, but we got the impression that he had some inkling that Geoff was trying to help him. Geoff firmly but carefully dislodged the wheelbarrow. The little bull stood stock still for a moment and then barrelled through the front gate and away down the hill.

The cows would often stand at the front gate staring at us with their beautiful soft brown eyes and chewing contemplatively. One very well-built cow, who we named Gillian, seemed particularly interested in us and would stand for a good half hour at the gate, looking thoughtful. One day, not long after the bull incident, the front gate let us down again and swung open. Before we could stop her, Gillian had seized her chance and ventured in, moving surprisingly quickly despite her wide girth. She proved harder to evict than the bull as she seemed totally unafraid of us. She stood solidly, gazing in an interested way at the front door, as we shouted, cajoled, and clapped to try to persuade her to move. We even tried pushing her rear end but it was like trying to move a Sherman tank. Eventually, Gillian stared at us dolefully for a few seconds and then just turned on her heels and calmly walked away. Needless to say, we fixed the gate that afternoon.

Another unwelcome intruder to the garden was grass. We were surrounded by rough grazing and peat bogs. This landscape produced an extraordinary range of beautiful wild plants. Amongst the short grass grew harebells and cowslips, tiny yellow tormentil, and delicate dog violets. The moist soil of the bogs was home to cuckoo flowers, cotton grass, and marsh violets. Geoff built a small wooden gate so that we had access through the back fence to Cae Bach. On a summer day it was fun to wander through the boggy meadow, jumping carefully from one grassy hillock to another and bending to stroke the fluffy white pompoms of cotton grass that decorated the meadow.

The downside of living in such an untamed landscape was that despite our best efforts, our garden probably housed the national collection of wild grasses. The worst was couch grass, which has strong roots and is difficult to eradicate. Our first vegetable beds were made by simply removing the turf and sowing directly into the soil. This wasn't a huge success as the couch grass quickly nibbled away at the edges of the beds, turning them back into turf before the seedlings had chance to grow very big.

We had little time to garden up at the cottage during the week. Beds that had been weeded one weekend would be almost as grassy a week later. Eventually we decided on a new approach. On the only part of the garden that was relatively flat, we built some raised beds edged with treated timber. To prevent the grass encroaching, we laid a weed membrane on the paths and covered them with gravel. These beds were our main vegetable growing area. To provide extra fertilizer we took occasional trips to some of the quieter beaches on Anglesey to collect a bag or two of seaweed. This rotted down beautifully and provided a good dose of nutrition for the plants.

In the first few years we were at Tyn-y-Bryn, the weather

was unusually warm. We grew sweetcorn and squash, different varieties of potatoes, and lots of onions. Carrots and kale did well and we even tried oriental greens like mizuna and Chinese cabbage. However, the slugs loved Chinese cabbage almost as much as we did, and with so much grass around, we had plenty of slugs. Despite almost nightly patrols and the enthusiastic use of beer traps, copper tape, and other weapons of mass mollusc destruction, damage limitation rather than slug eradication was the best we could manage.

Between the raised vegetable beds and the back gate into Cae Bach, the land sloped and there were several large rock outcrops. This area was not so good for orderly veg beds. Instead, we constructed irregular planting beds by filling in the hollows between the rocks and planting fruit trees and bushes. We grew gooseberries and red, white, and blackcurrants. These bushes were laden with fruit each year and we always started winter with a larder full of jars of fruit jam.

We planted several apple trees, one of which Geoff grew from a pip of an apple bought from the local greengrocers. The apple was delicious and we decided to try and grow a tree of our own. Against our expectations, the tree grew rapidly and was true to variety, producing a good crop of tasty apples. Alas, we hadn't kept a note of the name of the original apple, so we never knew what this wonderful variety was.

The cherry tree we planted by the little gate into Cae Bach grew tall and produced an abundant crop of delicious cherries every year. However, it was always a race between ourselves and the blackbirds as to who would get most of the crop. The birds always won; we never had more than about four ripe cherries to eat.

In the centre of the back garden, the ground rose slightly

and then levelled into a large flat rocky shelf. On one side of this shelf, the land fell away into a deepish hollow. We decided this was the perfect place for a pond. The water would attract beneficial wildlife like frogs that might help us control our slug population. Geoff began to dig. After working on a farm as a youngster, Geoff had developed strong back muscles and a penchant for heavy physical labour. The physical projects he undertook were ambitious and completed energetically. The pond he dug was large and deep. It had a shallow shelf at one end to provide access for wildlife and a sheltered spot for frogspawn. Geoff collected some large stones to fringe the pond and we filled it with aquatic plants.

We decided it would be a good idea to get a couple of fish to add to the diversity. Our tree surgeon friend Sam and his wife Sal knew of a good plant nursery that sold pond supplies and fish, so the four of us took a trip there one afternoon. We ordered coffee and homemade scones and took a table outside, overlooking the nursery's large fish pond.

'Are you sure the pond will be big enough for fish?' asked Sam.

'It's very large,' Geoff said. 'We'll show you when we get back.'

'But it needs to be deep too,' Sam persisted. 'You know how it freezes up there in the winter.'

'Wait till you see it,' I said. 'God, it's cold!'

I reflected that I was usually cold whenever we had lunch with Sam and Sal. They hated sitting indoors to eat and always persuaded us that it was warm enough to eat out. On this rather chilly day they had both been body-boarding and were now dressed in shorts and flip flops. I pulled my fleece closer round me and nursed my warm coffee cup.

Before we left we bought some marsh marigold plants

and four beautiful Koi carp for the pond. Back on the hill, the four of us headed for the back garden to release the fish. Sam stopped on the flat rock above the pond.

'Good grief!' he exclaimed. 'When you said you'd built a pond, I was picturing something ... well ... small.'

'We wanted a pond, not a puddle,' Geoff said.

'But it's huge!' Sam shook his head. 'I can't believe you did that.'

We weren't surprised at his reaction. Most people we knew, both locally and at work, seem dismayed at the amount of physical work our new life demanded. In modern times many people no longer have to work physically hard to live. Most of us do not have to chop wood, carry water, and hunt for food on a daily basis. In fact, the ideal is often to have enough money and enough labour-saving devices to lead a life of leisure divorced from any kind of manual work.

When we were up on our hillside hefting logs or stone, digging and planting, or just tramping about the hillside looking for wild flowers, we sometimes wondered why people joined gyms to become fit. Far better to have the wind on your face and the sun in your hair, and be spending your energy on a home you loved than on a treadmill in some stuffy gym. Both of us felt fitter and stronger than we had done in years. More importantly, we also felt a sense of confidence and self-reliance we had never felt before. Perhaps the physical convenience of modern life is a double-edged sword.

Meeting Gwyn had made us wonder if people were tougher and fitter in the past, when they had to do everything themselves. It is a popular assumption that our ancestors led lives that were 'nasty, brutish, and short'. However, estimates of lifespans in previous centuries are often skewed by infant mortality rates, which were undoubtedly higher than in modern times.

Inspired by our conversations with Gwyn, we had found some fascinating records in the local library of the inhabitants of the village in the 18th and 19th centuries. We were astonished to learn that at 90 years old, Gwyn was not unusual. Many of the villagers had lived well into their 80s and 90s, despite (or perhaps because of) a very hard life. The information only strengthened our conviction that money and modern comforts did not necessarily correlate with happiness. Unlike our life in the city, the challenges we experienced on the hillside felt energizing rather than stressful. It was true that we were still dependent on work, on commuting to the city, to earn a wage. But on the hill, we had autonomy, we were responsible for own well-being. For now, at least, it was a partial escape.

11

Despite our efforts, we were never going to be completely self-sufficient in food. Gwyn told us that when he lived at Tyn-y-Bryn the family grew only potatoes. They planted them not in the cottage garden but further down the hill, beyond the stream, in a sheltered little grove where the soil was more fertile. We often wandered down to this grove, which had a good feel about it. It was warm and peaceful on a sunny day and contained a huge upright stone studded with quartz. The stone looked like an old standing stone, but we suspected it was a natural formation. Nevertheless, it was an interesting spot to sit and dream.

We were determined to grow more than potatoes, even though our garden was eight hundred metres above sea level. To slow down the wind (and deter the troublesome sheep), we planted along the boundary fence a hedge of dog rose and hazelnut. We also tried to select varieties of fruit and veg that would cope with our difficult growing conditions.

The problem with some varieties of fruit and vegetable, particularly the ones widely available in supermarkets, is that while they may be suitable for large commercial growers they are less useful for the gardener. While qualities such as size and yield are important for commercial production, most gardeners are more interested in taste and ease of growing. Organic gardeners also need varieties that yield well without needing to be smothered in pesticides.

We spent time identifying and sourcing seeds of heritage varieties that could withstand the cold and damp growing conditions, avoiding F1 varieties so that we could save our own seeds to ensure a reliable supply in the future. After achieving good success with hardier vegetable varieties, we were keen to extend our growing range. We wanted tomatoes, sweet peppers, and chilli peppers. We longed for a warm place to start seeds off, safe from the slugs. We needed a polytunnel

There was only one suitable place for such a structure. Near to the east side of the house, sheltered by a huge rock on one side and two sycamore trees (Sylvie's sisters) on the other side, was a small piece of flat ground. This area was unsuitable for planting as the soil was particularly shallow but it was a good spot for a polytunnel. It wasn't ideal because of the overhanging sycamores, but it would have to do. However, we quickly realized it wasn't as simple as just ordering the right size tunnel. Our plot wasn't square but narrowed at one end. Neither was it level. Like everything else we built on the hill, the polytunnel had to be designed and constructed to fit the landscape.

Geoff built a wooden framework that fit the spot exactly, making some of the uprights shorter to accommodate the rise in ground level towards the back of the plot. We then ordered a plastic cover from a polytunnel manufacturer. We couldn't afford to buy shelves for the polytunnel so Geoff built some out of scraps of wood.

We sowed several different varieties of tomatoes and peppers and even tried growing a small grapevine. After arriving back from work, the first thing we did was race to the polytunnel and check the progress of our seeds. Having some cover enabled us to extend the short growing season and provide some protection for young vegetable plants before they were exposed to the mercy of the elements.

We put up a trellis to the west of the polytunnel and grew the rambling rose Paul's Himalayan Musk over it. This vigorous rose produced an effective barrier against the wind. It was the first purely decorative plant we put in, and we liked the way its small pink blooms wafted a gentle scent through that part of the garden.

However, despite the trellis, the polytunnel billowed like a huge sail when it was windy and was constantly battered during the gales. By the time our first plastic cover was nearing the end of its life, it was dotted with pieces of gaffer tape where we had tried to patch up the rips inflicted by the wind. Constant vigilance was also needed to make sure the bottom of the plastic didn't work loose from the stones and lengths of wood that we had used to secure it. Our cats took any chance they could to sneak inside the polytunnel and lounge on the warm seed trays, which they assumed were there entirely for their benefit. We threw out more than one tray of squished seedlings that had been abused in this way.

With no refrigerator and no freezer, we looked to traditional methods of preserving the food we grew. It is a pity that we had not at that time discovered natural methods of fermentation, which would have been perfect for our needs. However, we made chutney from tomatoes and squash and preserved basil and other herbs in oil. We had a huge rosemary bush in the front garden and we discovered that cider vinegar infused with rosemary is an excellent condiment.

As the apple trees grew, we had plenty of spare fruit so we regularly made cider. I found an old book on country wines and beers in a second-hand bookshop in Rhos-on-Sea, and we enthusiastically tried out several recipes. One of the best was nettle beer. We had an abundant supply of nettles on the hillside and regularly had to remove huge clumps of them from the bottom of the garden. We found they made tasty greens to add to dishes like pasta; a kind of poor man's spinach. And the beer that we produced from these 'weeds' was delicious, with a good body and a natural carbonation.

We also made damson wine from wild damsons we collected. If you walked further down the hillside, past Gwyn's potato patch and the quartz 'standing stone', you came to a little flat meadow next to a stream. Beyond the meadow was another stone cottage, smaller than our own and surrounded by pine trees. Some years ago, a local man had bought the cottage for his daughter and begun to renovate it. However, the daughter had decided, for reasons known only to herself, that she didn't want to live there, and the place had fallen into disrepair.

One summer, we wandered down there to discover signs that someone had been tidying the cottage and attempting some minor repair work. There were also the remains of a fire in the little grate. It turned out that some local teenagers had decided to spend their summer evenings there, accompanied by a boom box and a good supply of cider. They were obviously as keen on house restoration as they were on drinking, because the improvements to the cottage continued apace. However, after a couple of years, two of the teenagers went to university and the cottage was left once more in sleepy isolation.

Near the abandoned cottage were the remains of a little orchard containing damson and cherry trees. We took to visiting the orchard every autumn and collecting wild damsons with which we made wine, jams, and chutneys.

We discovered that the hillside provided many other foods for free, and we foraged enthusiastically. The hedgerows and fields were full of the large green leaves of garlic mustard, which tastes exactly as it sounds. We collected the delicate lemony-sharp leaves of wood sorrel and dug up little roots of pignut, which is like a small radish. Autumn walks in the woods produced plentiful supplies of blackberries and bilberries. We made sloe gin from the large black fruits of the blackthorn hedge near the track, and pink rowanberry jelly from fruit collected from the many rowan trees near the cottage.

One autumn, we discovered a huge mushroom growing on the trunk of Sylvie, the sycamore tree next to the cottage. It had a very large, rough, circular cap and was a rich brown colour. We consulted our forager's handbook excitedly. We came across many wild mushrooms on the hillside and in the woods but had never been able to reliably identify any of them. Consequently, we had opted not to sample any. It was a long way from our remote hillside to a hospital emergency room and it would be a shame to die for the sake of a good dinner.

However, this huge mushroom looked like none we had ever seen before. Our book suggested that there was only one mushroom it could be: Dryad's Saddle. Apparently, it was safe to eat and very tasty. There was certainly a lot of it. We collected a piece and lightly cooked it in butter and cautiously tried a small portion. It was delicious, full-flavoured, and meaty. The next day neither of us had experienced any bad reactions to the mushroom, so we harvested a larger piece and cooked that. We ate most of that mushroom over the next few days (leaving some for other critters) and when it had gone we mourned its loss. Although we looked each year, we never found another one. Shame.

When we could afford it, we replaced the tiny camping stove with a bigger calor gas cooker we found at a boat supply shop. For us, this new cooker was a luxurious upgrade. It had two gas rings instead of one and, marvel of marvels, a little oven. Its shiny stainless steel exterior shone in the dim light of our candlelit kitchen. Geoff was the chef of the house and had always cooked all our meals from scratch. When we moved to Tyn-y-Bryn, he had thrown himself into the challenge of cooking tasty meals on one gas ring. Now, with our new appliance, he managed to produce an astonishing range of food. He made elaborate stir fries with steamed dumplings, Mexican dishes with homemade tortillas, salsa and guacamole, pizzas, quiches, cakes, and biscuits.

As vegetarians, we sometimes found the range of food available in the local cafes and restaurants limited. If we had to eat out in the daytime, we opted for breakfasts (without the meat), as most cafes in Britain can at least rustle up a decent breakfast. A favourite haunt of ours was Sionedd's cafe in Betws-y-Coed. The small village has a genteel wooded charm which we liked. Its name means bede (prayer) house in the woods, and Betws' little church, with its huge yew trees and the nearby river bridge, was a good place to stroll and relax. At the weekend, if we had shopping to do or just wanted to go out and explore the area, we left the hillside early and made a day of it.

The process of driving down the track and negotiating several gates was time-consuming. We never just 'popped out' for one or two items; it was a waste of time and energy. If we were going to be out all day, we tried to start the day with one of Sionedd's magnificent veggie breakfasts and a large pot of Earl Grey tea. However, in summer, Betws heaved with tourists and walkers encumbered with huge rucksacks and hiking sticks, and the little cafe would fill up quickly. We had to leave the hill extra early to be at the cafe as soon the doors opened to be sure of getting a table. We were triumphant if we could get there in time and bag a seat and grumpy if we couldn't.

With the new oven, we started to make our own bread. Tired of the mass-produced bread offered by the local supermarkets, we had switched to buying sourdough bread from the health shop in Llanrwst. This was made by a local lady and, although expensive, it was delicious. However, her artisan loaves were very popular and sometimes sold out before we could buy any. Feeling under pressure to expand her business, the sourdough lady decided instead to retire. She had contacted a local bakery and suggested to them that they might want to take over producing the sourdough loaves. She had offered them her sourdough starter for free, explaining that she had a growing customer base so they would have no problem selling the loaves. However, the bakery had come to rely on mechanized production, and had no desire to diversify into handmade products.

One day the owner of the health shop, who we knew quite well, told us he had a gift for us. From under the counter, he produced a small plastic bag. It was a sourdough starter. He had told the sourdough lady of our enthusiasm for her bread and she had kindly given us some of her own starter, which was several years old, so that we could bake our own bread. We kept our starter on the marble shelf in the larder, where it seemed to be happy even in very hot weather, and made sourdough bread every week for years.

The more of our own food we produced the more disenchanted we became with commercial food. At work, for example, we stopped eating in the university canteen. This had always provided a good range of tasty and imaginative meals. When we could, we liked to eat there, although it was an expense we could have done without.

Our long commute meant that we left home early in the morning and got home late in the evening. By lunchtime, we were always starving and keen to have something substantial that would keep us going until our evening meal. However, the new management had evidently decided that the university canteen had to cut costs and make more money. Predictably, the quality and range of the food declined accordingly, although the prices did not. It seemed pointless paying money we could ill afford for food that was second rate, but the prospect of a lunch of limp sandwiches and a packet of crisps from the campus shop wasn't appealing either.

We decided that although we couldn't drive home for lunch, we could make more of an effort to devise interesting meals that were transportable. We devoted some time in the evenings and at weekends to preparing more substantial lunches. We packed plastic lunch boxes with slices of pizza and quiche, salads of rocket and lettuce leaves from the garden, little pasties of potato and soy mince, or tortilla wraps filled with beans and salad. We made chocolate brownies and muffins, or took homemade biscuits. In winter, we also packed a flask of soup, and we always took a flask of green tea.

Although the extra cooking and prep took up more precious time, it felt good having more control over what we ate away from home. It was too easy at work to race around like a headless chicken and miss lunch, or cram in a chocolate bar to save time. We had moved to Tyn-y-Bryn to seek a more mindful and authentic lifestyle. We were busier than we had ever been and poorer now we were trying to pay the cottage off. Ironically, but perhaps not surprisingly, we were doing more home cooking in our tiny primitive kitchen than we had ever done on the Rayburn in our large Liverpool kitchen.

Our previous life in the city, complete with mortgage and a monthly electricity bill, felt like it had happened years ago, to two different people. Now we had different goals: to be more independent of the system, to feel more grounded. We were reminded of this one sunny May afternoon when we hosted Gwyn and his family up at the cottage. The occasion was Gwyn's ninetieth birthday and Geoff had baked a celebratory cake for him. We brought the cake out to serve on the picnic bench under Sylvie, and one of Gwyn's daughters came over to help serve it. Her husband bit into his slice of cake then turned to her and said, 'Geoff's made this cake on a camping stove; why can't you make cakes like this in the Aga?'

I won't repeat here her forceful reply. We hastily changed the subject before a full-blown fight erupted!

12

Progress on the building work at the cottage was slow. We had resigned ourselves to the fact that it would take years to build the extension. We had all the stone we needed but it would take a while to save up for roof beams, flooring, and window frames. Work on clearing the site and moving stone to start the foundations had to be fitted in at the weekends, but our efforts were often thwarted by the challenging Snowdonia weather. It seemed to be an unwritten natural law that all the sunny calm days occurred during the week, when we were at work. Leaving work on Friday night, we would often drive from blazing sunshine into storm clouds and horizontal rain. A weekend sat by the fire listening to the wind howling outside was certainly cozy, but it got us no further with the building work.

We often suspected that our friends and family considered horizontal rain to be some kind of quaint Welsh myth, as they often smiled indulgently when we described our struggles with the weather. But if, dear reader, you know North Wales well, you will be nodding sympathetically at this point. On the hillside, the rain was often heavy and prolonged but rarely perpendicular. Because we were so high up, there was always movement, even if it was just a gentle breeze. On very windy days, the wind would throw the rain so hard that it became horizontal, or seem to blow in all directions at once. If we were outside, we might get rain in our faces and down the back of our necks simultaneously. If we were inside by the fire, we could watch the rain blowing horizontally past the window. This type of weather could often close in for days and was the subject of much local grumbling.

We occasionally visited the little town of Conwy, which we liked for its winding streets and little harbour. Conwy had an excellent fish and chip shop and we often walked down to the harbour and ate our chips sitting on the harbour wall. We often rounded off a trip to Conwy with a visit to the town's outdoor clothes shop. As we were regulars, we knew the owner a little and usually stopped for a chat. On one particular day, we had left the hill in bright sunshine only to find that a squall had blown up in Conwy. We raced to the outdoor shop for shelter through horizontal rain that was threatening to turn into hail.

Inside, we commiserated with the shop owner about the atrocious weather.

'We've only just had the west wall repointed,' he complained. 'The rain, it just drives itself into the mortar no matter what we do!' He hit the palm of one hand with the fingertips of the other to emphasize his point. 'How does it do that, do you think?' he asked plaintively.

We thoroughly sympathized with his despair. The horizontal rain did indeed find its way through every little crack and crevice. Most of it seemed to end up in our little hallway. The cottage had a perfectly good front door made of solid wood, and a small porch. However, the porch was shallow and was open to the elements, so the horizontal rain had no trouble finding its way under the door. In wet weather, we often returned home from work to find the slate flagstones in the hallway under a centimetre of water. What we needed was more protection from the rain and wind.

Geoff therefore dismantled the porch and rebuilt it, adding stone to make the structure deeper. This gave us a useful space to store wellies and raincoats. He added a small window to each of the side walls, constructing the window frames himself. We took off the existing front door and hung it on the front of the porch. We replaced it with a new front door that we happily paid nothing for. We spotted the door one morning in a skip outside a house near the university. It was made of thick wood with glazed panels comprising the top half. The house owner seemed surprised when we asked if we could take the door but readily agreed. She watched us curiously from the window as we loaded the door into Buffy. We were thrilled at our acquisition; the new door was perfect as it let more light into the hallway, which now thankfully stayed nice and dry.

Another major improvement to our well-being was the installation of hot and cold running water to the kitchen. We bought a new calor gas water heater for the kitchen, and started to work on a way to plumb water into the house rather than having to walk down the hill to collect it each day. The spring was quite a way downhill from the house, so we had to figure out a way to pump the water one hundred metres uphill, and find somewhere suitable to store it when it got there.

After some searching, we found and bought a powerful 12-volt pump. We placed the pump in the spring box enclosure and connected it to a battery powered by a solar panel. The water tank we had in the kitchen was small and had to be filled every day. We didn't want to have to pump water up every day, so we bought online two very large cold water domestic water tanks. It was always a problem getting large items delivered to the cottage as our post box was at the bottom of the hill about half a mile from the house. Therefore, we got the water tanks delivered to my parents' house near Liverpool and ferried them over one at a time in Buffy.

We often thought of Buffy as our carthorse because we seemed to spend a lot of time carrying heavy loads to and fro: coal, logs, water containers, gas bottles, furniture. With the back seats down, she could easily accommodate one of the water tanks. We transported each one up the hill to the rocky outcrop we had selected as the best location for them. This outcrop was by the house and just behind Sylvie. It was sheltered by her overhanging branches and little visited by the sheep. It was also high enough to allow the water to be gravity fed to the house.

Geoff enclosed the tanks in a wooden framework and insulated it with polystyrene. We hoped that this would be sufficient to stop the water freezing in winter. Now all we had to do was run a water pipe from the tanks to the pump down at the spring. This was easier said than done, as the pipe had to cross Tomos' land and so would be vulnerable to trampling by the sheep and cows. We used standard water pipe but enclosed it in thick, strong plastic piping to give it some protection. We had to position the pipe so that it followed the shortest route between the water tanks and spring, but so that it avoided the main trackways of the sheep and cows. It was practically impossible to bury the pipe as the soil on the hillside was so shallow. Instead, we ran it through the bracken patches behind the barn, where the animals rarely went, and covered any exposed pipe with stones.

Ironically, the only damage to the pipe occurred not from the animals but from Tomos' son Alun. We returned home from shopping one Saturday afternoon to find that the section of pipe near the barn had been severed. It was annoying; another thing to fix, and it was too late to go back out and start hunting for replacement water pipe. Luckily, we still had plenty of water in the tanks so we didn't need to pump any more up that day. It would have to be fixed the following weekend. However, that evening there was a knock at our door. It was Alun, come to apologize for breaking our pipe. He had accidentally run over it with his quad bike. When he realized what he had done, he drove to Llanrwst to buy a piece of replacement pipe. While we had been preparing our evening meal, Alun had returned on his quad bike and quietly fixed the pipe.

This kind of undemonstrative support was typical of our gentle neighbours and characteristic of our small community. Even though we weren't at the cottage all the time, we tried to help out where we could. One spring day, on our way to work, we came across a very young lamb on the track. It had squeezed its way through a small gap in the hedge of one of Lewys' fields. Lewys' small dairy farm was near the village but his land extended to the bottom of our hill. Both the lamb and its mother, who was still in the field, were calling plaintively and upon seeing Buffy, the lamb looked ready to bolt down the track. I stopped the car, and without thinking, Geoff leapt out, grabbed the lamb, and flung it bodily back over the hedge!

We called at Lewys' on the way to work to tell him about the gap in the hedge. We suspected that our students wouldn't have believed us if we had told them of some of the odd challenges we sometimes faced to get to work.

Although Buffy was invaluable for bringing all sorts of large or heavy loads up to the cottage, some things were too large even for her and without the convenience of home deliveries, we had to devise our own methods of transportation. One such occasion occurred when we rather rashly bought two enormous plastic tanks to use as compost bins. We found these on a freecycle site and couldn't resist them. They were ex-orange juice containers and came with free delivery (to the bottom of the hill of course). We just had to work out a way to get them up the track, through the wood, and across the hill.

Although huge, the tanks were light and initially we thought we could roll them all the way up. The track through the woods was relatively smooth so we managed to roll each one up the hill. However, the track across the field was another matter. The rocky parts of the track sent the first container lurching into the gorse bushes, and we almost got it stuck in the mud when we reached a damp patch. We gave up trying to roll the containers and fetched our sturdy wheelbarrow. After several attempts, we managed to tie a container to the wheelbarrow. It was a precarious arrangement, but sufficient to get our load back to the cottage. We chose the site for the containers very carefully because we knew we would never be able to move them again!

For most of the year, the track next to the cottage was too wet to risk bringing Buffy down it, so we used our trusty wheelbarrow to transport many heavy loads from the car to the house, including logs, coal, and gas bottles. However, when we decided to buy an Aga, we had the sense to know that we needed more robust transport than the wheelbarrow.

When we had moved from our Liverpool house, we had been sorry to leave the Rayburn and had dreamt of installing a similar range cooker at Tyn-y-Bryn. A solid fuel stove that we could cook on and that would warm the whole house would be ideal. However, our decision to pay the cottage off in five years meant that money was tight. We couldn't afford a new range, and the second-hand reconditioned ones we had seen advertised were also out of our price range.

Then one day, our friend Sam announced that he knew of a second-hand Aga that was for sale. We were having breakfast at the Alpine cafe in Betws. It was a good place to linger over breakfast and the Sunday papers, and its large windows looked out onto the little railway station, providing a good opportunity for people-watching. Sam and Sal, it turned out, knew an elderly couple who were keen to sell their solid fuel Aga in order to install a gas-fired one. The price was very reasonable so we agreed to go and take a look that afternoon.

We often speculated that Sam and Sal knew practically everyone within a 30-mile radius. Sam's job as a tree surgeon meant that he had worked for many people in the local area. Added to that was the fact that the pair were very sociable and had an enormous circle of friends and acquaintances. It was an odd fact that many of these friends were really quite eccentric, a fact that Sam and Sal revelled in. We met a number of these characters over the years and had been regaled with tales of the antics of others.

For example, one afternoon they took us to meet Bob, a friend who they described as 'keen on home improvements.' Bob was a retired physics teacher who lived in a rambling old house in the hills, surrounded by tangled woodland and a garden full of strange wooden sculptures he had made himself. We admired the garden but what he really wanted to show us was his 'project'. He led us to a large concrete building near the house which looked a bit like a bunker. In here, he said, he was building a machine. What sort of machine we wondered? His explanation was lengthy and utterly impenetrable. To this day, none of us have the slightest idea what Bob was building in that bunker of his.

Whatever it was, Bob was wary to the point of paranoia about possible spies. The flat roof of his bunker had a large panel that at the flick of a switch slid back to reveal the sky. When we asked what it was for, Bob looked solemn.

'So I can keep an eye on them,' he said. 'They fly over, you know?'

We didn't.

'They fly over and try to take pictures,' Bob insisted. 'But with this,' he demonstrated the skylight again, 'I can play them at their own game. I can watch *them*!'

'Who are *they*?' we asked Sam and Sal as we drove home from Bob's.

'No idea,' Sam said cheerfully. 'We like Bob so we just agree with him so as not to offend him. By the way, he grows marvellous radishes.'

We sometimes wondered whether Sam and Sal considered us 'mad friends' too. Did they entertain their other friends with tales of the crazy academics who lived off the system in a primitive house on a hill? At least, we thought, we were in good company. North Wales, like other mountainous areas of the UK, seemed to attract people who were trying to escape something or looking for a refuge, people who had different dreams or were trying to live a different sort of life. Just like the Celts centuries ago, many modern folk had decided for various reasons to 'run for the hills'.

We wondered sometimes why Sam and Sal had not bought Tyn-y-Bryn when it had been on the market. They were renting a house and often bemoaned the fact that houses in the local area were too expensive. However, we came to realize that they had different priorities to our own. They were both more extraverted than us; they liked living in the valley where they had easy access to their friends and to the coast. They liked our hillside and thought the cottage was cute, but we knew they weren't keen on the sort of extensive renovation that Tyn-y-Bryn needed. Like most people we knew, Sam and Sal would have hated the inconvenience of living in a house off the system, even if it meant being able to own that house outright. We understood their feelings, but thought they were crazy to spend their money on things like an expensive pizza oven for their garden. I expect they thought we were crazy to live without a bathroom and central heating.

The Aga that Sam and Sal took us to see was perfect for our needs and we agreed to buy it. We just had to find a way to get it up to the cottage. Yet another of Sam and Sal's eccentric friends, Dan, came to the rescue. Dan was a laconic Welshman with a dry sense of humour. He also had a small flatbed truck that he insisted could cope with the steep slope near the cottage. We were doubtful, but the ground was dry and Dan was keen for the challenge. We took the heavy doors and lids off the Aga to make it lighter. Dan had a trolley with a lifting mechanism and this was invaluable in getting the stove onto the truck.

The journey across the rocky track was rather hair-raising, even, we noted with amusement, for Dan. Like most people, he was a little horrified at just how bumpy the track was, and we stopped several times to make sure that the ropes securing the Aga were tight. We eventually got the truck to just outside the cottage without mishap. However, the narrowness of the front door and kitchen door, and the sharp angle between them, meant that the trolley was no use in getting the Aga into the kitchen. It took some time, but with a combination of brute force and determination, Dan, Geoff, and Sam manhandled it up the kitchen step and onto the concrete plinth that Geoff had built.

It was wonderful to see an Aga in our little kitchen. It needed some cleaning up and we had yet to install a flue for it, but its very presence spoke of cozy winter evenings to come. It stood next to the little calor gas cooker, solid and reassuring, its cream doors glowing in the candlelight.

The Aga seemed to us a symbol of permanence, a sign that we were going to be here for a long time. It provided a strange contrast to the utilitarian camping cooker, but we considered both essential. Living off-grid in a remote place meant that we had to have multiple systems to fall back on. The calor gas stove was ideal for immediate use but if the price of gas skyrocketed, or if Buffy broke down and we couldn't collect gas bottles, we now had the Aga, which we could run on scraps of wood foraged from the hillside if necessary. We were beginning to realize that to be truly independent and live successfully off the system was only possible by using multiple strategies and planning for all eventualities.

13

From the earliest days at the cottage, we were enthusiastic 'preppers'. Nowadays, with rising prices, supply problems, and the effects of the COVID-19 pandemic, many people are embracing prepping as a sensible way of safeguarding essential supplies and preparing for the worst. Back then, it was more unusual and another characteristic that was considered odd by our family and friends.

However, we had quickly realized that living on the hillside required a level of preparedness that we had not needed before. The remote location meant that it was infeasible to quickly 'pop out' to the shops; if you forgot an item, you had to do without it in the short term. Because of the extreme weather, we lived with the almost constant possibility of becoming housebound because of deep snow, flooding, or other problems. And with no Internet access, shaky mobile phone coverage, and the difficult access, we couldn't rely on home deliveries of food or any other essentials. As a result, we had to be self-reliant and very organized to ensure we didn't freeze or go without food if we were cut off for a week or two. We always had a full complement of gas bottles, coal, logs, candles, gas mantles, and food (for us and for the cats) at Tyn-y-Bryn because we couldn't afford not to. We also made sure that we had a good set of tools and other equipment. If anything went wrong with the plumbing, heating, or power, we had to fix it ourselves.

An interesting couple we met inspired us to take our prepping to a higher level. We met them through a strange set of circumstances, which I will try to describe here. As in most universities, our psychology department sometimes received enquiries from members of the public seeking specialist guidance or advice.

One day, Geoff received a phone call from a Mr Scott, who lived near Llandudno. His wife's father had died recently and the couple had taken in the father's budgerigar, to which he had been devoted. Then odd things had started to happen. Mrs Scott starting hearing strange noises when she was alone in the house, such as doors slamming upstairs when she was downstairs, and the radio switching itself on and off. This had developed to the point where Mrs Scott was afraid to be in the house alone. In addition, she had become afraid of Dinky, her father's budgie. Her father had spent much time talking to Dinky, and the bird had a wide vocal repertoire. He talked constantly and his utterances were like a stream of words and other noises, delivered with varying intonation and cadence. Listening to Dinky chattering away to himself all day, Mrs Scott had become convinced that the bird was possessed by evil spirits, and that his vocalizations contained threatening messages directed at herself.

We visited the Scotts several times to talk to Mrs Scott and, at her request, made some recordings of Dinky's utterances to reassure her that, though complex, they had no sinister content. Mrs Scott could not bear to have the bird in the house, so they had placed his cage in their large garage.

The first time we saw the garage, we were astonished.

110

Lining each wall were metal storage shelves that were crammed with all nature of goods: tinned food, bags of flour, rice, pasta, sugar, soap powder, toilet rolls, and cleaning supplies. Mr Scott gave us a tour, and explained his belief that it made financial and practical sense for everyone to have a large supply of essentials in store. The Scotts lived in a perfectly ordinary modern house on a large estate. We never learnt the reasons why Mr Scott had become an early adopter of prepping, but we were impressed by his philosophy and by his efforts.

We left the Scotts with more than just tips on prepping. Mrs Scott's state of mind seemed to improve after she talked to us about her anxieties and her underlying grief for her father. However, she was adamant that she would not feel completely comfortable in the house until Dinky was gone. Ideally, a good home would be found for the bird but if not, Mrs Scott was prepared to have him euthanized. Thus it was that we found ourselves driving back from Llandudno one afternoon with a budgie on the back seat of Buffy.

Because of their unusual powers of speech and imitation, we often attribute mind or intention to birds like budgerigars and parrots. They are 'liminal' creatures, not just dumb animals but not quite human. Because of this, throughout history and across many different cultures, 'talking birds' have been both revered as god-like and demonized as devilish. In fact, some research on such birds suggests that the complexity of their communication and thought is much greater than previously believed. After analysing Dinky's communication patterns, we concluded that he was probably talking to comfort himself, repeating over and over the words and phrases that his owner had taught him, and embellishing them with new phrases of his own. In short, he was lonely and afraid, and missing Mrs Scott's father.

We bought the bird a larger cage and installed him in the sitting room, where he sat and chattered all day (one of his favourite phrases was 'Dirty Gerty,' uttered with some feeling!). In the daytime, when the cats were safely out of the way, Dinky was allowed to fly around the sitting room. He liked to perch on the big mantelpiece over the fire, but when he could he preferred to sit on my head and chew my hair, or perch on Geoff's shoulder and nibble his ear. We found him to be a clever and affectionate bird, and gave him as much attention as we could. However, although he undoubtedly had a better life than he did in the Scott's garage, we felt guilty that he was on his own all day while we were at work.

However, Dinky's story had a happy ending when we heard that my brother-in-law's mother had lost her beloved budgie. We told her about Dinky and she eagerly offered him a home. As she was retired and at home all day, she gave Dinky the company and attention he craved.

Despite our new prepping drive following the tour of Mr Scott's garage, we had a basic problem: storage. Our small kitchen and larder held only the essentials; we had insufficient cupboard space to store more than a week's supply of food. Also, we needed somewhere dry to store tools, logs, and garden equipment. We had been keeping these in the tiny pigshed near the cottage but it leaked and had no door, so the sheep often wandered in to nose around. We needed a shed. A big shed. And, like the polytunnel, it would have to be built from scratch to accommodate the contours of our rocky site.

We found a suitable plan for a simple shed in a book and started sourcing timber for uprights and roof beams, chipboard for the floor and walls, and tongue and groove cladding to cover the outside walls. We decided to build the shed close to the east wall of the cottage. The land sloped upwards away from the house, so the shed wall closest to the house would have to sit on uprights to ensure that the floor was level. The gap between the shed and the house was about a metre and would provide the perfect space to store logs. We measured up and Geoff set to work, with me as labourer's mate.

The structure Geoff built was a cut above the usual tool shed. At 3.5 metres by 2.5 metres, it was more like a tiny house. This effect was enhanced by the shed's three large wood-framed windows and a wood and glass door. These came from a garden summerhouse owned by Geoff's mother. She had asked us to dismantle the summerhouse for her and was more than happy for us to take away the doors and windows. Geoff fitted a wooden deck to the front of the shed to provide a dry overhang, and roofed the whole shed with slate tiles we found in the outbuilding. We also fitted a cat flap into the front wall of the shed so that the cats had somewhere dry to shelter when we were at work. However, we soon realized that their front door, like our own, let in the insidious horizontal rain. So they soon had their own little porch, which opened to the side to shelter the cat flap and prevent it blowing open in the wind.

My father couldn't wait to see the shed once it was finished, and he and my mother drove over specially to inspect it. He loved construction of any kind and had followed the progress of the shed with interest. When he saw it, he looked astonished.

'I didn't think it would be this big!' he said. Then something seemed to dawn on him. 'How did you run the power tools?' he asked. 'Did you buy a generator?'

'No,' Geoff said. 'I used hand tools.'

'Hand tools! For the whole thing?'

'Of course,' Geoff said.

My dad shook his head slowly, as if with astonishment. 'Hand tools!' he said. 'Well I never!'

He was still shaking his head with disbelief as he was driving away that afternoon.

The extra storage the shed provided turned our small plot into more of a homestead. We now had a warm(ish) dry space in which to store extra provisions as well as crops such as onions, which we braided and hung to dry in the shed. We gleefully stocked up on dry goods, cleaning supplies, and household items such as candles and firelighters. We were now able to buy some foods in bulk, which cutting down on both cost and shopping trips.

One of our favourite shopping haunts was a small but eclectic grocery store near Abergele. Norman and Joyce, the owners, were quite a bit older than us and had moved to North Wales thirty years ago. They were nearing retirement but loathe to sell their little shop. They sold large sacks of flour, oats, and rice, as well as foods difficult to find elsewhere at that time, such as tahini and miso.

Norman was an enthusiastic user of health supplements and herbs, and stocked a good range of dried herbs and tinctures. Geoff and I both had an interest in complementary and alternative medicine, so we grew many herbs in the garden and used some simple home remedies for common health problems. For example, I suffered from migraines and made my own herbal tincture from yarrow leaves, which was very effective. We grew lots of calendula (marigolds) in the garden as they attract beneficial insects. The flowers have an anti-inflammatory effect so I used them to make a soothing skin cream. And the rosemary bush in the front garden provided a good supply of leaves for both cooking and to make a nourishing hair and scalp oil. Norman had an encyclopaedic knowledge of herbs and supplements, so we often compared remedies and exchanged advice with him.

The one thing Norman hated about the shop was the annual stocktaking. For a couple of weeks each year, he and Joyce would be in a distracted state as they struggled to get their records in order. One day, Norman announced that he had managed to secure funding from the council to invest in a barcoding system for the shop. Once every item had a barcode, he explained, the new computer would keep track of sales and stock, making life much easier. They were eagerly awaiting delivery of the new equipment, and Norman was thrilled to finally be part of what he considered a shiny new age of tech-savvy shopkeeping.

Over the next two weeks, a technician scanned every item in the shop to produce a database of barcodes. Norman was jubilant and gave us detailed accounts of the progress. But when we called in at the shop a few weeks later we were greeted with chaos. Every surface was covered with haphazard piles of goods and the wooden counter was a mess of paperwork. Norman and Joyce seemed to be in the middle of an argument and looked extremely flustered. Red in the face, Norman came to the counter to greet us. We asked him if he was stocktaking and he groaned and nodded. But why the chaos? we asked. Surely the new barcoding system was in place now? To our surprise, Norman put a finger to his lips.

'Shhh!'

'What?'

He checked the door nervously to see if anyone was about to come in. His voice dropped to a whisper.

'We don't talk about that,' he said. 'It's down there.' He gestured to a space under the counter.

'What, the barcod—'

'Shhh!'

'You're not using it?'

115

He shook his head solemnly, then leant forward conspiratorially.

'We couldn't,' he whispered. 'It's ...' he lifted his eyebrows to the heavens and shook his head despairingly, 'impossible. But don't tell anyone!'

We couldn't help smiling when we had left Norman to his stocktaking. He was so excited about the promise of automation for his little shop, but installing the system had obviously been a lot more complicated than he had anticipated. He now had two things to worry about: the stocktaking and the council calling round to demand their grant back!

14

If moving to the cottage was an extreme lifestyle change for us, it was even more so for our cats. Leaving an urban garden and the noise of the city for forty acres of wild Welsh hillside redolent with all kinds of scents must have been a strange experience for them.

We had two cats when we left Liverpool. The youngest of the two, Bunna, had not been with us long when we moved. Bunna had appeared out of nowhere one day and had refused to leave. I had taken some students on a field trip to Anglesey and was away for a week. When I returned, Geoff announced that we now had three cats instead of two, and introduced me to Bunna, a friendly little tabby with huge paws and a knowing expression. We asked around and put a notice in the local pet shop, but nobody claimed Bunna, so she stayed. We always joked that she must have been shocked when we suddenly moved to Wales; life in the country may not have been on her agenda. Or perhaps she had an inkling of our impending move when she adopted us and decided that she, too, was going to escape the city.

Over the last 30 years, we have shared our homes with ten cats. We never meant to have so many but we seem to always be encountering cats who are lost or abandoned, or have become waifs and strays for other reasons. In

Liverpool, we already had two cats when Bunna arrived. These had been acquired from some people squatting in a house near Sefton Park. The hippies, as we called them, had adopted an unneutered cat and so had found themselves with a litter of pure black kittens that they were keen to be rid of. We agreed to adopt one kitten, a female.

A few days later, we learnt that homes had been found for all the kittens except one, a male who was the runt of the litter and not in the best of health. We decided we had to go back and bring him home with us.

Mephlie, as we named him, was indeed undersized and spent three days under a bookcase, fleas patrolling his little anxious face, refusing to come out. Poppy, his sister, enjoyed racing over to the bookcase and thwacking any part of him that was within reach. However, it didn't take long for them both to settle in well. Considering his unpromising start, Mephlie surprised us by living to an impressive old age; he was seventeen when he died on the hill.

I should say something about the naming of our cats. We always tried to pick names that reflected the character of each cat. This meant that their names often changed as we got to know each animal better. For instance, Mephlie was originally Mephistopheles, named for his black colour and cunning nature. However, he quickly showed himself to be a sweet-natured and unassuming cat rather than the devilish scamp his name implied. His name therefore quickly morphed into the diminutive Mephlie. The opposite happened with Bunna. We originally named her Honey or HoneyBunny, because of her yellowy-orange colouring. It soon became apparent that she was nobody's honey; she was a self-possessed and tough little cat, and had a wise, knowing air about her.

We also amused ourselves by occasionally bestowing on the cats unusual names that seemed to capture specific aspects of their character. The evocative folk names of wild herbs were good for this purpose. So Mephlie was occasionally known as Germander Speedwell, which we thought aptly described his rather dignified air, and Poppy as Bogbean, a nickname that made us chuckle and that we thought fitted her rather mischievous nature and dubious hygiene habits.

Some scholars insist that assuming that animals have personalities is anthropomorphic; that is, it involves attributing human-like qualities to nonhumans. However, research over the last twenty years shows that ratings or descriptions of animal personality are generally consistent, and accurately reflect observed behaviours of those animals. Moreover, anyone who has shared their life with a companion animal knows that concepts like personality and intent are necessary to explain the complexity of their animal's responses.

All of our cats had distinct personalities and adapted to life on the hillside in different ways. After their morning meal, they would trot off purposefully to their own particular haunts. When we went for walks, we would sometimes happen unexpectedly upon one of them, perhaps crouched silently by the stream watching the little eddies caused by the breeze, or lying half-hidden in the branches of the old oak, like small spirits of the hillside. They loved the place as much as we did. We still have an old photograph of Mephlie crouched watchfully on a rocky ledge. His green eyes reflect the many greens of the landscape around him: the lichen on the rock, the moist grass, and the leaves of Sylvie in the background.

By the time we moved to the cottage, Poppy had died. One of our neighbours in Liverpool insisted that they had seen rats in their back garden, and frequently left out food laced with poison. Headstrong and curious, Poppy always had her eyes set on far horizons and often investigated the neighbours' gardens. We even caught her a few times strolling down the middle of the main road at night. When she and two other cats in the neighbourhood died suddenly, we suspected that our neighbour's careless use of poison was to blame.

We hoped that Mephlie and Bunna would be safer in Wales. For the first week or so, we confined the cats to the cottage so they could become familiarized with the place. This was a stressful experience for all of us, as the cats spent hours patrolling the boundaries of each room and mewling. It was equally nerve-wracking when they were finally let out; all we could do was hope that they wouldn't lose their heads and get lost in their new wild environment. It was entirely in character that upon first venturing into the great outdoors, Mephlie wandered into a large patch of nettles and stung his eye. In contrast, Bunna sashayed off down the hillside as if she owned the place and wandered back that evening completely unperturbed.

Few other domestic cats roamed our hillside. The exception was a stray tomcat known as Thon. A huge smoky-black animal, Thon was rarely aggressive towards other cats but he did have a reputation with the ladies. We sometimes encountered exotic felines on the track at the bottom of the hill. Val, a neighbour who lived in the village, bred Bengal cats and occasionally one would escape and wander up our track. We grew familiar with those cats that were the worst offenders for breaking out and usually managed to scoop them up, put them in the Jeep, and quickly drop them off at Val's. Thon was Val's nemesis as he had managed to impregnate two of her pedigree Bengal beauties.

One summer, we decided to find a companion for Bunna. Although Bunna's exact age was a mystery, we knew she was a lot younger than Mephlie. We were worried that when Mephlie died, Bunna would be on her own when we were at work. Although she was a very confident cat, we thought she might feel lonely. So we decided to look for another cat to adopt.

One day, we had called at Val's to drop off Amber, a golden-haired Bengal whose sweet face and innocent expression concealed a will of iron and a devious nature. We knew Amber quite well. She was one of Val's most accomplished escapees and broke out about once a month.

'Oh Amber!' Val said when we took her back home. 'Not again!'

Val led us into the kitchen and put the kettle on. An ex-psychiatric nurse, she had given up nursing to breed cats. However, we noticed that Val's home had more than a touch of the clinical about it. In the large kitchen, the worktops were absolutely devoid of any objects: no utensils, no jars, no toaster, nothing. Similarly, in the sitting room, there were no ornaments or decorative items of any kind. We could see why. Cats were everywhere. They patrolled every surface, including the kitchen counters. They lounged on chairs or on purpose-built cat 'trees'. They commandeered the windowsills, the sofa, and the space in front of the fire. All were in top condition, and despite the number of animals, the house was spotless. It was clear that Val ran her home and business with the same military precision that she must have employed in running a psychiatric ward.

We finished our tea and headed outside to the car. As we did so, we saw a figure hurriedly duck into an outbuilding.

'Colin!' Val called 'Come and meet Geoff and Marie.'

Val explained that Colin was an old friend of hers. He seemed pleasant but very nervous. His watchful eyes darted constantly from side to side. We guessed, correctly as it turned out, that he had been a psychiatric patient.

'Before you go, come and have a look at these,' Val said.

She led us to a little outbuilding. Occupying a large pen was a beautiful dainty-looking female cat and four tiny kittens. The mother was Lola, one of Val's prize breeding Bengals.

'They're gorgeous!' I exclaimed. 'Are you selling them?'

'No,' she said. 'I could if I was unscrupulous because their markings are almost perfect. But I won't. They're Thon's.'

Despite her vigilance, Val had been unable to prevent a liaison between Lola and Thon and now had four crossbreed kittens to find homes for.

'You don't want a kitten do you?' she begged. 'They're free to a good home.'

'As a matter of fact, we do.' Geoff said.

We returned a few weeks later to collect the kitten. Val knew we were calling that afternoon but there was no answer at the back door. We strolled to one of the outbuildings to look for her. As we neared the barn door, Colin emerged, a startled look on his face.

'Hi Colin,' Geoff said. 'How are you?'

'There's nothing wrong with me!' Colin shouted and hurried towards the house. 'Val!' he yelled. 'The psychologists are here!'

Val had evidently mentioned to Colin that we were psychologists at the university, so Geoff's casual enquiry after his health had thrown the poor man into a panic! We felt guilty for worrying him but Val was sanguine about it.

'He's fine,' she said. 'It's good for him to be challenged. He needs to learn not to over-react!'

Just as in Liverpool, we ended up adopting two kittens instead of one. All of Lola's litter had found homes except a little male. It seemed a pity to leave him on his own, so we took him too.

We named our exotic kittens Zuleica and Silvio Manuel,

after the Spanish sorcerers in one of Carlos Castaneda's books. As usual, their given names mutated as we got to know them better. Zuleica became Zullie and Silvio Manuel became Sibby, which eventually became Bibby. Mephlie seemed bemused by the new additions to the household, but largely ignored them. We hoped that Bunna would get along with them, as we had adopted them with her in mind. She hated them. She was never aggressive towards the kittens; she simply regarded them with utter disdain.

One day, Bunna just disappeared. For three days, we trekked across the hillside calling her but to no avail. Then one day, I was doing something in the kitchen. Suddenly, I had a strange feeling of absolute certainty that Bunna was very close. So much so, that I bent to gaze out of the kitchen window at the slope leading down to the house. A few seconds later, a small shape came hurtling down the slope to the house. It was Bunna. We were overjoyed to see her, and she seemed none the worst for her escapade. However, a few weeks later, she disappeared again. This time she didn't return.

There must have been something in the air that year, because shortly after Bunna left, Bibby did his own disappearing act. One Saturday morning, he failed to appear for breakfast. The weather was dry and fine so we assumed he had just got distracted on one of his hillside patrols, and that he would shortly reappear. However, by Monday morning, when we had to leave for work, there was still no sign of Bibby. Each evening we called him in vain. By Friday night we feared that he too had disappeared like Bunna.

However, working in the garden on Sunday afternoon, we heard a strange cry. Slinking in the front gate was Bibby, mewing plaintively. The little cat was slightly bedraggled and a little thin, but otherwise unhurt. But he had a wild haunted look in his eyes that we had not seen before. We didn't know where he had been or what he'd been up to, but whatever it was it had thoroughly spooked him. The episode seemed to have cured his lust for adventure because he never wandered off again.

Unlike her brother, Zullie had a thirst for danger from an early age and was always in some sort of trouble. If any of the cats stomped on a wasp and got stung, it was Zullie. If there was any squabbling over food or comfy spots by the fire, it was usually started by Zullie. All the cats had their own cozy bed in the shed, where they spent the night. Not content to curl up in her own bed (and often in one of the other cat's beds) Zullie spent some nights exploring the forbidden areas of the shed, such as the high shelves on which we stored sharp tools, oil cans, and any potentially dangerous chemicals like paint stripper. Zullie considered it her personal mission to check out all such shelves. Unfortunately, she seemed to lack the poise and grace that cats are supposed to have. Her combination of clumsiness and recklessness meant that she very often fell off things. We rarely saw it happen, but could always tell when Zullie had been rummaging because the shed would look like a small poltergeist had visited. We suspected that the chipped tooth she appeared with one morning had been sustained in a fall during one of her shed sorties.

From being quite young, Zullie regularly wandered off for whole days, and sometimes for a couple of days at a time. One clue about her activities during these outings was provided when we chatted one day to our neighbour Mrs Roberts, whose farmhouse we had stayed at when we had viewed the cottage. Mrs Roberts sometimes walked across the fields as far as our track, which bounded the Roberts' farm. We happened to be on the track that day, washing Buffy. Zullie was pottering about near us, trying

124

to shove her nose into the bucket of soapy water. The cats rarely saw strangers up on the hill, so we were surprised when Zullie ran over to Mrs Roberts and allowed herself to be lifted up and petted. Seeing our look of surprise, Mrs Roberts laughed.

'Oh, we know each other quite well, this poppet and me,' she said. 'She often comes to visit me.'

We learnt that Zullie regularly trekked over to the Roberts' farm. Mrs Roberts had figured out that Zullie had an owner because of her good condition and general tameness. When Zullie left the farm one day Mrs Roberts had followed her out of curiosity, and had realized that Zullie was probably owned by us.

'When she turns up, I tell her to go home you know,' Mrs Roberts explained. 'But she won't until she's had an hour or two sitting on my knee in front of the fire!'

That wasn't the only thing that Zullie had managed to extract from the kind-hearted Mrs Roberts. Apparently, she had her own box of cat treats at the farm and often received choice scraps of meat and fish.

'Oh and she does like her warm milk when it's cold!' Mrs Roberts finished.

We stared goggle-eyed at Zullie, who gazed innocently back.

'Little cow!' Geoff said later when we were back in the house. 'Mrs Roberts must think we starve her!'

'How can she?' I said. 'That cat has got a definite paunch! I suppose it's no wonder; she's been on double rations for months.'

Knowing about Zullie's double life, when she vanished a few months later, we called at the Roberts' to see if she was there. But she wasn't. Mrs Roberts was as worried as we were, and said that she hadn't seen Zullie for over a week. She never returned, either to us or to the Roberts'. We were left hoping that she had simply wandered a little too far and had found a comfortable home with someone else, which, knowing Zullie's winning ways, we suspected she had.

Of all our cats, it was Mephlie who made the hill his own and who seemed most in his element up there. Although he liked his home comforts, he sometimes preferred to be outside in the evening, even in winter, rather than curled up in front of the fire with the rest of the cats (yes, a heap of cats on the hearth when one is trying to put more logs on the fire is definitely an accident waiting to happen, but their collective will was stronger than ours). From his inauspicious start in a squat in the city, Mephlie developed into a confident, independent animal who spent his days wandering across the hillside like a small shadow.

Mephlie died one winter's evening in front of the fire. That day, he had completed his usual patrol of the garden boundaries and had settled in a sheltered spot in the garden to sleep. However, he had not looked well all day, so we brought him inside and made him a bed by the fire. It was sad to say goodbye to him but we were comforted by the fact that he had had a peaceful natural death.

A strange thing happened the following day. Mephlie had a peculiar plaintive call, which sounded exactly like a crow cawing. In fact, we sometimes called him our little crow. At the weekend, when we rose a little later in the mornings, Mephlie would sit underneath our bedroom window and make his odd cawing call. We often joked that if he could, Mephlie would have climbed up to the bedroom window to stare impatiently in at us. Luckily, although the cats often sat on the downstairs window sills, there was no vantage point to allow them to access the upstairs sills.

The morning after Mephlie died, we were woken by a loud cawing sound. This was accompanied by a soft tapping at the bedroom window. Mystified, we gently pulled back the curtain. There on the windowsill was a large black crow. It sat watching us calmly before giving a last caw and flying to perch in the tree opposite the house. We had seen crows occasionally on the hillside but none had ever ventured close to the house before, let alone tapped on the window. That crow stayed by the house for nearly a week. Several times, it tapped on the bedroom window, and sometimes on the kitchen window (another favourite haunt of Mephlie's), calling loudly. When we left the house, the bird would call from the tree and swoop over the garden. We couldn't help but think about our little crow, the gentle black cat who had been our companion for so long. Perhaps after all those years on his beloved hillside, Mephlie just couldn't bear to leave.

15

As the cottage became a little more comfortable, we welcomed more visitors up to the hill. While most people were charmed by the cottage, its location prompted mixed reactions. It was always fascinating to observe how people responded once they were on the hillside. Several friends and relatives seemed a little shocked at the remoteness of the place; they looked round at the rolling hillside and the enormous view and went very quiet. In contrast, one friend said that he wished he lived in such an isolated location because it would allow him to smoke his cannabis in peace! Some people were unnerved by the silence. Without the sound of traffic or neighbours, and no television chatter in the background, the quiet could be absolute, especially at night.

The only thing that disturbed our peace was the occasional fighter jet screaming overhead, *en route* from the RAF Valley base on Anglesey. They were annoying because they appeared out of nowhere and the noise was tremendous. We suspected, probably unfairly, that they used the cottage as a landmark and liked to fly over it.

One day, after three planes had made us jump out of our skins, Geoff lost his temper and phoned RAF Valley to complain. The woman who took his call seemed genuinely astonished that he considered the flyovers a negative thing.

'I don't understand what the problem is,' she said.

'The problem is that they are too noisy and they fly far too low. One flew over yesterday and we could clearly see the plane's undercarriage and the pilot!'

'Really?' she said. 'Oh yes, they are marvellous aren't they?!'

Geoff gave up.

Some visitors were enthusiastic about the landscape but fell foul of the rugged terrain. An aunt of mine fell in the stream at the bottom of the hill. My mum had decided to take her for a walk across the hillside to show her the view. Shortly after they had left the cottage, we heard squeals and shouts. We looked down the slope to see them both ankle-deep in the stream and doubled over with laughter. They returned to the cottage soaking wet and giggling like ten-year-olds. On another occasion, Geoff's sister-in-law tripped and fell into a gorse bush. We spent that afternoon extracting gorse spines from her hand. My niece had rather a better experience. She was four or five at the time and was utterly bewitched by the garden. She ran round joyously, picking wild flowers and chasing the many butterflies.

Our lack of a bathroom and spare bedroom meant that we had few overnight guests. However, at different times, both Geoff's mother and mine made use of the sofa bed in the sitting room and came to stay for a weekend. They were bemused to be presented with a head torch to wear so that they could navigate round the house. Both mothers enjoyed the peace of the hillside, although it was unfortunate that when my mother stayed, Zullie and Bibby were still small kittens and so were temporarily confined to the house. My mother's peaceful slumber was periodically wrecked by the sound of small paws pounding up and down the stairs just outside the sitting room door!

Although we were used to the rather primitive state of the cottage, we were aware that our living conditions were not to everyone's taste. Therefore, when our neighbour Beti and her husband Will, who lived down the hill in a more modern house, visited the cottage one dark autumn afternoon, we found ourselves apologizing as they squinted to stir their tea in the dim light of the sitting room.

'No need to fret,' said Will cheerfully. 'I'm used to doing things by firelight in this house. Did you know I was born here?'

We didn't, and begged him to tell us everything he could remember about living in the cottage as a child. We found out from Will that several other villagers had also been born at Tyn-y-Bryn.

'This place is like the cradle of the whole village!' remarked Geoff.

Other visitors were less complementary about our lack of modern facilities. One friend became exasperated when trying to look at one of our books.

'Oh, I can't see this!' he exclaimed. 'I don't know how you put up with it!'

When Geoff's brother and his wife visited to help us install a wood-burning stove in the sitting room, they were very polite about the cottage, but looked at us with a mixture of pity and concern, as if we were ever so slightly insane. I suppose being asked to help heave a cast-iron stove across a remote windy hillside was sufficient grounds to doubt our sanity.

We had decided to take out the small fireplace in the sitting room and replace it with a stove. Although we loved the open fire, it was undersized for the fireplace and logs often rolled out of the grate onto the hearth. The sitting room fire was also the sole source of heat in the cottage, so we needed something that would warm the whole house. We searched the adverts in the local newspapers for a second-hand stove that would suit our budget and finally found one that sounded suitable. The woman selling it lived near Llangollen, so we set out one sunny Saturday to view the stove.

I have fond memories of visiting Llangollen as a child with my Aunty Bronwen. She would take me and my sister to one of the town's teashops and buy us orange juice and cake. I can still smell the synthetic scent of the little lilac bottles of 'Welsh violets' perfume she used to buy us, and hear her trying to teach us some of the Welsh words she knew.

The drive from the hill to Llangollen went through some beautiful countryside and we occasionally made the excursion, often calling at an interesting plant nursery on the way. We had discovered the nursery by accident one day. We were walking past a large old house that had a huge bottlebrush tree in the garden. It was in full bloom and pink blossoms hung over the garden wall. We stopped to admire it, not noticing the elderly lady pruning a rose on the other side of the low wall. She saw us and smiled, gesturing for us to come to the gate. We were a little surprised when she invited us inside and proceeded to give us a tour.

It was just the sort of garden we both liked: wild, rambling, and full of unusual plants. As we neared the back of the house, the garden rose up in stone terraces. These were crammed with plants of all sizes. We noticed that many had labels on, and realized that they were for sale. We had stumbled across the plant nursery from heaven. The prices of the plants were ridiculously low; evidently the owner was an enthusiast who had decided to make a little extra cash from her passion for plants. She was never going to get rich from her plant sales but she was obviously more than content to spend each day in her garden.

For us, the main draw of Llangollen itself was the bookshop, which occupied a huge Victorian house on the high street. The shop was enormous and rambled over four storeys. Each floor was stuffed with books; they were crammed onto rickety bookshelves and piled onto chairs and windowsills. Books overflowed from the rooms onto the landings and were stacked in the stairwells. It was quite a climb up to the top floor, where the rooms got smaller and more attic-like, and the books older and more esoteric. It was the perfect place to spend an afternoon, and easy to lose track of time while wandering the labyrinthine corridors. In a perfect combination, the ground floor of the bookshop was a cafe that sold simple but well-cooked food. We always ordered the same thing: egg and chips, bread and butter, and an enormous pot of tea. This was enough to keep us going for our usual three-hour browse in the bookshop.

We had arranged to view the stove in the afternoon, which allowed ample time for a visit to the bookshop for food and a lengthy browse. After tea and homemade scones, we were shown the stove, which looked perfect for our needs. It was large and almost new; the woman selling it was a widower and had decided that it was too much work to feed a log-burning stove throughout the winter. She wanted to replace the stove with a gas fire and was keen for a quick sale. We arranged to collect the stove the following weekend.

Luckily, the weather was dry and the ground was hard. We parked Buffy close to Tyn-y-Bryn, and Geoff and his brother managed to heave the stove into the sitting room and position it next to the fireplace where it was to stay until we had time to remove the old fire. To celebrate (and recover), we all headed to the pub in the village for a well-earned meal.

The removal of the old fire, two weeks later, turned out to be a filthy job. The small grate sat inside a large slate surround, which when we began to dismantle it, turned out to contain a huge amount of cement and concrete infill. We must have removed about forty bucketfuls of this material, which left a persistent layer of dust on everything in the sitting room.

The hearth itself consisted of huge thick slabs of slate, one of which was unfortunately cracked. This we replaced with a slate slab we had found in the pigshed before moving the stove, with much difficulty, onto the hearth. We had measured the length of the chimney carefully and bought some suitable flue pipe. Now it was just a matter of feeding the pipe through the chimney and connecting it to the stove. What we naively imagined would be the easiest part of the job turned out to be the most difficult. The pipe slid most of the way up the chimney easily, but then got stuck near the top. Even with both of us pushing, it wouldn't budge. Geoff eventually climbed up onto the roof. He reached inside the chimney and started pulling the pipe, while I stayed on the hearth and pushed. Whether it was because the chimney narrowed slightly towards the top or the pipe was marginally wider at one end, it took us almost two hours to inch the wretched thing into position. But finally it was done. We just hoped that we never had to replace the pipe ever again!

It was wonderful to finally have the stove in situ. Geoff replastered and painted the back wall of the inglenook where the slate surround had been and we cleaned up the hearth until the slates shone. The last thing we needed to do before using the stove was to repair the old chimney pots. However, when Geoff went onto the roof to examine them again, he realized they were beyond repair. We would have to replace them with new pots. This was a problem, because that weekend we had a rare house guest. This was Neil, a friend of ours who had newly taken up gardening and was keen to try growing his own vegetables. We had suggested that he visit and take a look round our garden, and had even promised him some young tomato plants to take home with him. However, we could tell he was a little worried at the thought of having to 'rough it' in a cottage with fewer home comforts than he was used to.

Although it was May, it remained cold in the evenings and at night. As Neil would be sleeping in the sitting room, we needed to get the stove working. With only a couple of days before our guest arrived, we hastily toured the local builders merchants until we found pots of the right size. Geoff then spent the best part of two days on the roof cementing the new chimney pots into place. In fact, Neil arrived earlier than expected and caught Geoff on the roof, making a final check that the cement had set before the inaugural lighting of the new stove.

'When you said you had a few jobs to do before my visit, I didn't think you meant fixing the roof!' Neil said.

'Oh the roof's fine,' Geoff called down. 'It's the chimney pots I've been working on. In fact, now that you're here Neil … I don't suppose you could give me a hand? The ladder's over there … you're okay with heights aren't you?'

Poor Neil's eyes popped out of his head, and he began to stammer out an excuse before he realized that Geoff was joking.

To our relief, the stove performed beautifully and we were glad to wave Neil off on Sunday evening with his tomato plants but (thankfully) without hypothermia.

16

With the new stove, the cottage became more comfortable in the winter. The house was so small that the warmth easily filtered through to the bedrooms and we no longer had to cope with iced-up bedroom windows. The next big task was to try and generate some of our own electricity so that we could have a few lights and run some small appliances like laptop computers. Today, there is a wide range of solar panels, wind turbines, and associated products available to suit all budgets. This was not the case fifteen or twenty years ago. I remember trying to buy 12-volt leads in a major high street electrical goods store and watching the assistant dissolve into giggles. We spent much time searching the Internet and emailing suppliers to find what we needed.

We decided that a system consisting of four 100-watt solar panels and a wind turbine would provide about 400 watts, which would be sufficient for our modest needs. The panels could not be positioned on the roof, as the roof was slate and old and we didn't want to chance any damage to it. Also, we knew that the roof might need some major repair work in the future, work that would have to be done carefully, as there were bats nesting in the roof space. There was an area at the side of the house where the panels would be safe from the sheep and could be placed at the correct angle. However, we needed a dry space to store the batteries relatively close to the panels. The only solution was to build another shed.

Geoff used the same design he had used for the other shed to build a small version on the same principles. Although we managed to salvage some suitable windows, we couldn't find a door so Geoff built one. Like the big shed, the little shed had to stand on a wooden framework because the land sloped very steeply in this part of the garden. We hoped the new shed would not suffer too much from the wind as it was in an exposed position facing the mountains, although it was protected from the north by a huge rock outcrop.

There was no chance of getting the solar panels delivered to the cottage so they had to be sent to work. The university porters were used to receiving large packages for us, but even they were astonished at the size of the panels. It was obvious they were dying to know the contents of the huge boxes but we decided it was easier to let them guess than to get into a discussion about our off-grid domestic arrangements.

We had been unable to find a suitable wind turbine in the UK so we ordered one from the USA. The propeller blade was compact but despite this, we were a little shocked at how heavy the turbine was. A pole to support the propeller had proved difficult to find but we had eventually located a firm in Llandudno who could make one to our specifications, along with the necessary fittings to attach the propeller to the pole. We transported the four-metre pole back to the cottage on Buffy's roof. We tied a flag to the front of the pole and a flag to the back and just prayed that we weren't stopped by the police on the way.

We attached the wind turbine to the pole easily enough but getting the pole upright in position was another matter.

It was too heavy for the two of us so my father and uncle offered to come over and help. My father was an instrument technician and adored working with any kind of machine. In many ways, he thought we were quite mad to have chosen to live off the system but he was always interested in the latest developments at the cottage and eager to be involved where he could. My uncle was happy to help and was also keen to put his new Range Rover through its paces on our rough track. I still remember his rather shocked expression as he climbed out of the vehicle after a bone-shaking ride down the track. However, with their help, the new wind turbine was soon in place and functioning and we celebrated over homemade apple pie.

We had looked forward to having constant power from the turbine because it was almost always windy on the hill. But we were disappointed. We had bought a powerful turbine so that it could handle the frequent strong gales. However, the turbine was so heavy it remained stubbornly motionless if the wind was light. In contrast, when it was very windy, the turbine spun wildly and made a very loud humming sound. As it was positioned at the front of the cottage not far from our bedroom window, the noise was hard to ignore on windy nights. We would lie awake in the dark listening to the humming get louder and louder and imagining (quite irrationally) the propeller detaching itself to go spinning wildly across the hillside in the direction of Moel Siabod.

The solar panels were more of a success. We installed a solar controller and batteries in the new little shed near the panels. All we had to do then was to run the electrical cable from the panels into the house, but we encountered the same problem as with the water pipe: the ground was too shallow to properly bury the cable. We therefore adopted the same solution: we encased the electrical cable in thick water pipe and buried it shallowly as and where we could. In some places we just had to cover it with rocks and hope that it didn't get damaged.

After much searching, Geoff managed to source some 12-volt LED wall lights. We fitted these in every room in the house. They used relatively little power but gave off much more light than the gas lamps and candles. It was wonderful to have enough light to read properly by. However, one downside of the greater illumination was that it revealed aspects of the house we had previously not noticed, such as the damp in the corners of the sitting room, the mouldy bit of carpet under the table, and (to our horror) the soot that coated the sitting room ceiling. In the cozy candlelight, the ceiling retreated into warm shadowy dimness. Now that we had more light we realized why. Candles were by no means a clean way of lighting a house. The gas lamps also generated patches of soot on the walls.

We began to get an insight into characteristics of pre-modern life that we hadn't previously considered. Before the use of electric lights and modern heating systems, people must have been more tolerant of the inevitable soot and damp. We had once visited a local historic house and been shown round by a tour guide. He showed us the huge inglenook fireplace and pointed out a series of long burn marks on the beam above the fireplace where in the seventeenth century, the house's owner had cleaned the poker. The same marks were visible above our own fireplace. Our modern sensibilities consider these more gritty aspects of living unacceptable. Although we were in some ways sorry to lose the warm candlelit glow we had grown used to, we had to accept that a programme of redecoration and refurbishment was badly needed.

As well as lighting, our new off-grid system provided luxuries such as the use of a stereo and laptop computers, which we ran using an inverter that converted the 12-volt DC power into 240 volts AC. The stereo was very low wattage and we were able to run this almost continuously when we were at home.

The computers and lights drew more from our modest system. We therefore had to be mindful of how much power we were using at any given time. For example, if the lights were on in the kitchen then we used our head torches to pop upstairs rather than switch on the hall light. This felt natural rather than inconvenient; we had both got used to either pulling on a head torch or expertly feeling our way round the house in the dark. Indeed, even after installing the lights, we often forgot to flick a light switch and wandered round the house in the half-dark. After living so long without them, we never took either the running water or electricity for granted; rather, it always seemed a minor miracle that we had these luxuries and that we were responsible for providing them.

There were of course some appliances we were unable to run on our small system. An electric kettle and an iron were out of the question as they were too power-hungry. However, our camping kettle worked perfectly well on the gas hob, and we were more than happy to be free of the chore of ironing. We sometimes missed having a vacuum cleaner. However, we found that the use of a stiff brush and a good dustpan did an admirable job on the floors, and in the summer we scrubbed the rugs and dried them in the garden.

Eventually, as a backup, we did purchase a petrol generator. This allowed us to run power tools and also a vacuum cleaner. However, as using the vacuum required going to the little shed, starting up the generator (which was temperamental), running an extension lead from the shed to the house, and passing the lead through the sitting room window, we used the vacuum only occasionally.

Although we could have run a television, we chose not to. There were many more interesting things to do than watch television for hours. However, we did like to watch films and this was easily achieved using a laptop with a CD DVD drive. Despite not having a television we received constant letters from the television licensing authority asking why had not registered with them. We sent many replies explaining that we did not have a television. They obviously didn't believe us because the stream of letters continued, each warning of the dire consequences of not having a license and threatening a visit from an inspector. We lived in hope that an inspector would one day manage the hike up to the cottage and planned to provide this intrepid person with a slap-up tea as a reward for their resourcefulness and bravery. Alas, we never had a visit and can only assume that either no inspector was dispatched or that one is still wandering about lost on the hillside.

17

Modern psychology rarely looks beyond the human world when considering the causes of mental health and mental illness. Much is written about the influences of family and society on health and happiness but the role of the more-than-human world is rarely explored. In childhood we recognize that nature is a place of mystery and meaning, full of hidden significance and magical beings. Children enjoy a sense of connection with nature akin to that probably enjoyed by our earliest ancestors.

Some scholars have used the concept of 'biophilia' to explain this feeling of connection. Biophilia is a universal innate tendency for a sense of connection and affiliation with the natural world. Its expression is dependent on culture, learning, and life experiences. A growing body of research shows that a rich relationship with nature is fundamental to physical and mental health.

Unfortunately, for many people this relationship is impoverished or frustrated. Our modern, fast-paced, urban lifestyle often distances us from nature. Consumer culture and technology promise fulfilment. But rather than feeling content, many of us in modern times feel more disconnected, distracted, anxious, and dissatisfied than ever before. In a society that increasingly values money and status, we are more and more cut off from those things that supported and nurtured our ancestors: community, religion, nature.

Some psychologists and scholars have argued that our cognitive development, well-being, and even our very humanness is dependent on our connection with nature. For example, the psychologist Paul Shepard suggests that human cognitive development, self-identity, and imagination are dependent upon understanding the similarities and differences between ourselves and non-human species. In other words, we define ourselves only in relation to others, or as the ecologist David Abram puts it '...we are human only in contact, and conviviality, with what is not human.'

If this is the case, then psychologists must look beyond the individual and the family to understand the roots of psychological sickness, and try to help people to establish a sense of connection that nourishes them.

Our own sense of disconnection in the city and dissatisfaction with our hectic lifestyle that prompted our move to Wales also inspired us to try to develop a course that explored the connections between nature and psychology. An important part of the course was a week-long field trip to Anglesey to allow the students to more practically engage with the topics discussed on the course. We hoped that by taking the students off campus and into the 'wilds of Wales' (as one student put it) they might gain a more embodied understanding of the role of the natural world in human psychology.

To encourage the students to engage more deeply with the topic, we used group dialogues rather than lectures. The use of dialogue in science was recommended by the physicist David Bohm as an alternative to the usual argument and debate that characterizes scientific discourse. The process of dialogue is a better vehicle for exploring people's thoughts, preconceptions, beliefs, and biases within an open and honest exchange. Participants are encouraged to suspend their judgement and develop the skill of active listening, with the aim of reaching a more nuanced understanding of the dialogue topics.

We booked an outdoor activity centre on Anglesey that was perfect. It had simple but roomy sleeping accommodation and a large kitchen and dining room with space for group discussions. Although the centre provided optional cooked meals we decided that bringing a supply of food and asking the students to help us prepare home-cooked meals was more in keeping with the principles of the course. This suggestion was generally greeted with enthusiasm, although one or two students looked doubtful.

'I only eat chicken and chips,' one student announced. 'I don't like vegetables or fruit. Just so you know.'

Another student who we knew liked his pints asked why we couldn't just go to the pub for dinner each evening. Our vision of harmonious evenings cooking as a group began to look a little ambitious. However, after some discussion, a compromise was reached. Our chicken and chips girl was told that her favourite dish could feature on the menu as long as she agreed to at least try one or two vegetables. We also agreed that a few after-dinner visits to the pub, which could be accessed via a small secluded beach, would do no harm.

We hired a minibus to transport the students from the university to Anglesey, and one of our mature students agreed to drive it. We were going to lead the way in Buffy after picking up a week's supply of fresh fruit and vegetables. We ordered these from Rhys' greengrocer's shop in Llanrwst and also stocked up on basics like flour, rice, tea, and coffee. Rhys helped us to load the Jeep with the produce and then wished us luck.

'I think you're going to need it,' he said 'Look at those clouds!'

We glanced apprehensively at the sky. It was full of heavy dark clouds that had an odd yellowish tinge. Typically, heavy snow had been forecast that morning. Neither of us relished a drive down the country lanes of Anglesey in thick snow with a minibus of students in tow.

'Let's get going,' said Geoff. 'We might at least be able to get there before it starts snowing heavily.'

Thankfully, we made it to the centre before the weather turned. However, we had barely unpacked and made coffee before the snow began. The students sat gloomily looking out of the French windows at the swirling snowflakes. We were at least off campus which was a welcome change for the students. But it would be a shame to come all the way to Anglesey and not be able to take advantage of the wonderful environment.

Luckily, the next morning, the weather was fine and dry and it stayed that way for the whole week. We took the students for hikes and conducted teaching sessions on the grass outside the centre. We went for walks on the beaches and watched the students explore the clear rock pools.

One evening, we ate dinner on the beach. With the help of the students, we prepared some food and carried it down the steep path to the beach. We built a small fire on the sand and toasted marshmallows for dessert. Outside the confines of the classroom and lecture hall, the students relaxed and we had some lively discussions about how our environment changes our thinking. Some of the students revealed how they had spent little time outside the city. One student kept gazing at the mountains and saying 'I've never been anywhere like this before!'

Some students were intrigued that we lived not far away and pressed us for information about our life on the hillside. For the sake of privacy, and because we knew it would probably shock them, we were deliberately vague about the details of our very basic living conditions. One student asked us why we had a Jeep.

'It's not very ecological is it?' he said. 'I mean, why don't you get a smaller more ecological car, or get the train into work?'

We explained that we needed a four-wheel drive vehicle to get anywhere near the house and pointed out Buffy's 'walking boots', as we called her off-road tyres. We also told him how we had recently had Buffy converted so that she could run on LPG gas, which was not only cheaper than petrol but supposed to be better for the environment.

'But why not just live closer to work?' the student persisted.

Been there, done that, we thought!

We tried to explain our aim to live more minimally and (eventually) become debt free, leaving out the fact that we also hoped to be able to work less or choose a less stressful job in the future. But we could understand that student's point. We had no mains services at the cottage and we never used air travel, so Buffy was our only ecological 'footprint'. However, having a long commute to work wasn't ideal either for the environment or for our finances. We spent a lot of money on the car, both in terms of fuel and frequent maintenance, to ensure that we had a reliable means of getting to work and returning home.

Like many aspects of our new lifestyle, the long commute was a compromise. We couldn't afford to give up work just yet and neither could we afford a small cottage in the countryside nearer work. So we had no choice but to live further afield. However, there was another factor that made having a car essential. Like many rural areas in the UK, North Wales lacked an extensive public transport system.

We had once spent the best part of an entire day trying to get to work via public transport. Buffy had had to have some unexpected major repair work and we found ourselves without a car for a day or two. We obtained a train timetable and figured that it would be possible to get the train from Llanrwst to Llandudno, and then pick up a connecting train to work. The local bus from the village down the hill to Llanrwst was so infrequent it was almost mythical, so we got up extra early for the long walk down, carrying waterproof coats and our work bags.

When we got to Llanrwst station, we found it was deserted. There was no ticket office, so we assumed we could buy tickets on the train. We were in good time for the next train to Llandudno, which unfortunately failed to materialize, as did the one after that. Eventually, after two and half hours, a train appeared and we were able to continue our journey. Upon reaching Llandudno station, we found that we had missed our connection. After waiting for about an hour for the next one, we learnt that it had been cancelled and that there would be a replacement bus service ... which also didn't turn up. We gave up and got a taxi back to Llanrwst.

By then, it was late afternoon and dusk was falling. By the time we began the walk back up to the village, it was almost dark. People were coming home from work and the road out of Llanrwst was busy. Shortly out of Llanrwst, the pavements disappeared and the road ran between fields of sheep and cows. We found ourselves walking in the grass verges to avoid the cars, which sped along recklessly. At regular intervals, we flattened ourselves into the hedgerows, worried that we were about to be mown down. It was terrifying. I let out the occasional shriek and Geoff pulled me to his side. By the time we reached the quiet turnoff up to the village we were both a little shaken. We reached the cottage at about 7 p.m., after a long fruitless day. We had learnt our lesson: it would have been better to hire a car than to battle with the unreliable train service and the 'wall of death' walk on the Llanrwst road.

On the morning of our departure from Anglesey, the whole group looked tired, and we knew why. Late last night, there had been the sounds of a loud argument and then a scuffle. Two of the male students had been vying all week for the attention of the same girl, and the rivalry had obviously finally come to a head. We could tell who was involved by the evidence of torn tee-shirt necks and the odd bruise. Despite the night's disruption, we deliberately said nothing to the students over breakfast. After all, we had been encouraging them all week to be more self-reflective and to think more deeply about their own actions and prejudices. It seemed like the two rivals had learnt something during the week, because after breakfast they made up their differences and apologized to us and the rest of the group for the late-night disturbance.

As we packed up the minibus, the sun was strong and the coconut smell of the gorse drifted by on a light breeze. Most of the students were gloomy at the prospect of going back to the city. As it was a Sunday, we were driving home to the hill rather than accompanying them to the university. We would be back on Anglesey in just a few days as Buffy was booked into a garage for a major service that we were praying wouldn't reveal too many problems.

'Is it those mountains where you live?' enquired one girl. We nodded.

'You're so lucky,' she sighed. 'You must be really happy there.'

'Well, it's not so easy in winter,' replied Geoff. 'But yes, we are happy there.'

We reflected that we were indeed lucky to be driving back that day to such a special place. But there was no doubt that it was a happiness that was hard won.

18

Summer was our favourite time of the year to be up at Tyn-y-Bryn. For three weeks or so we would spend every day on the hillside, working on the cottage, sitting in the garden, and reacquainting ourselves with the landscape. We could go for days without seeing another soul, content in our isolation. Pottering around the hill in scruffy shorts and sandals, tanned and relaxed, we would feel ourselves slowing down, becoming more grounded, more mindful. The stress of work and the hustle of the city seemed like a different life.

On those warm, fragrant days, it was easy to imagine that time had stopped and we were back in an earlier age. Half-dreaming in the garden, one could easily mistake a faint noise on the track as the sound of a horse's hoof against stone as someone rode home from the village. And that soft rustle from the kitchen might well be Gwyn's mother, Eleanor, wrapping her butter to sell at tomorrow's market, or preparing supper for the family.

Gwyn had told us that to supplement the family's meagre diet he would trap rabbits, which were plentiful on the hillside. But by the time we moved there, the wild rabbit population had dwindled; those that were left were safe from us as we were vegetarians! However, as the garden became more productive, we began to think of ways we could be more self-sufficient.

One obvious possibility was chickens. We had the space, and plenty of grass. It would be wonderful to have our own eggs. However, we had occasionally seen foxes on the hillside and knew it would be difficult to deter them from the garden. We were away at work during the day and often didn't return until after dark. Our friends Sam and Sal had recently lost almost all their hens to a marauding fox and they were at home much more than us and had a large dog who patrolled the garden (though not very diligently, apparently).

After some reading and a lot of thought we decided that chickens would be too much trouble. One of our favourite sources of inspiration at that time was John Seymour's book on self-sufficiency. We loved Seymour's idea of a self-reliant homestead, complete with chickens, goats, and a system of crop rotation. However, we didn't have the luxury of being at home all week to tend the place, and our scrubby, rocky hillside garden looked nothing like the flat ordered smallholding pictured in Seymour's book. Moreover, when we thought about it, we realized that neither of us wanted to be farmers. Work at the university might be trying and stressful at times but at heart we were scholars: we wanted to be free to think and write. Life was hectic enough as it was without the addition of a flock of squabbling hens and a couple of bossy goats.

It occurred to us that one food item we regularly bought that could be produced at home was honey. We loved honey and good quality honey was quite expensive. Why not acquire some bees and become self-sufficient in honey?

We bought a couple of books and began researching the idea. Bee hives required only occasional maintenance, and we were sufficiently far away from any neighbours to not cause any nuisance. And there were forty acres of wild flowers, gorse blossom, heather, and other food sources for the bees to enjoy. Beekeeping seemed like the perfect addition to our modest homestead.

We started to look for beekeepers in the local area who might be able to provide us with a starter colony of bees, but met with little success. Eventually, we located a company that provided both starter colonies and all the equipment necessary to keep bees. The only trouble was, it was in Lincolnshire.

So one hot spring day, we found ourselves driving through the country lanes near the ancient city of Lincoln. The flat, fertile landscape in this eastern part of the UK seemed strange to our eyes, accustomed as they were to the mountains and woods of North Wales.

After several wrong turns, we finally found the beekeeping place and after a pep talk by their helpful staff, loaded up Buffy with our beekeeping supplies. Into the back seat went two beekeeping suits, hats, and veils; a smoker and other small tools; and the two solid wooden hives we had bought. Into Buffy's shady boot went the most important item (and the one we were most nervous about): a wooden box containing a small starter colony of honey bees. The box had ventilation holes but these, we were assured, were too small for the bees to escape through. Nevertheless, we had a fraught ride all the way back to Wales. Both of us kept glancing in the rear-view mirrors to check for any sign of escapees. The prospect of speeding down the motorway with a car full of furious bees was not appealing.

Our little colony seemed none the worse for their journey and were soon happily installed at the bottom of the garden by the hawthorn hedge. Beekeeping proved to be rewarding and productive. We loved sitting in the garden with binoculars watching the bees returning to the hive with the little sacs on their legs full of pollen. We became good at guessing where they had spent the afternoon by the colour of their pollen: a haul of orangey-red pollen showed that they had been foraging on the gorse flowers and yellow pollen told us that they had been working the evening primroses.

We were a little nervous when we had to inspect the hives for the first time. We carefully donned our beekeeping suits and fussed with hats, veils, and gloves to be sure we were fully protected. We filled the smoker with small twigs, lit it, and waited for the smoke to develop. A few puffs of smoke through the hive entrance would render the bees placid, as they would assume that the hive was on fire and busy themselves with collecting honey rather than thinking about stinging us. Then we could safely open up the hive and check the 'supers' for brood and honey. We hoped that neither of us was allergic to bee stings, as in the event of anaphylactic shock, it would be impossible to quickly obtain medical help in our remote location. Happily, neither of us were, so our beekeeping activities did not prove to be fatal.

In time, we acquired another two hives, as our initial bee colony was vigorous and swarmed several times. The first swarm was difficult to catch, as the bees settled on a high branch of an alder tree, tightly packed around the new queen. We couldn't reach them even with a ladder. Eventually, we managed to fix a container to the end of a long wooden pole, detach them from the branch, and house them in a new hive.

Our bees were generally a peaceful colony and we gradually got used to dealing with swarms. And they produced a lot of honey. The honey harvest was a time-consuming and sticky task. Because we had limited power, we bought a manual rather than an electric extractor. The supers were placed into the extractor and then the handle turned as fast as possible to spin the supers. This flung the honey out of the comb and onto the walls of the extractor, from where it could be scraped off. In our tiny kitchen, the extraction process and the subsequent clean-up was a herculean task. But it was worth it. Seeing a row of jars filled with the sweet amber honey was heart-warming and it was the best honey we had ever tasted. Our friend Sam swore that our honey was a cure-all for a whole range of ailments.

One day, we were tending the bees when we realized we were being watched. A small group of walkers were on the track beyond Cae Bach and were gazing at us curiously. We must have made an odd sight in our beekeeping suits and hats, bending over the hives in a haze of smoke. One of the group aimed a camera at us and another bent down and picked up a small child, pointing us out to the toddler. They must have been charmed to be confronted with this image of a bygone age during their walk and must have felt, like us, that time had somehow stood still on this remote Welsh hillside.

But time had not stood still and the hill had changed. Although the landscape looked as if it had not changed for centuries, the habitat that Gwyn had known as a child was long gone. The cuckoos and woodpeckers could still be heard and the harebells and Welsh poppies waved in the grass under the trees, but with the rise in the number of sheep many species had disappeared. Overgrazing over the last few decades had produced a landscape of cropped grass, which easily became parched in the summer. With the disappearance of the wild rabbits, the kestrels had left. Gwyn had warned us to be careful of adders in the long grass; alas, there was hardly any long grass left for them to hide in. As the farms had got bigger, the itinerant shepherds, like Gwyn's father, had left and the cottage economies had dwindled.

We were aware that our search for a pristine rural landscape untouched by the modern hand of progress had been unrealistic. All landscapes, except the very remote, are shaped by human habitation, animal husbandry practices, and changing climate patterns. Our desire for an older way of life rooted in the seasonal rhythms of nature had drawn us to this small rural outpost. But finding an authentic way of living in the modern world was difficult. Our own small cottage economy, in terms of the food and honey we produced, was modest and supplemented by our university salaries. We had respect and sympathy for our neighbouring farmers, who faced many challenges in eking out a small living from the difficult terrain.

We grew familiar with the patterns and practices of our adopted community. We no longer panicked when we smelt burning and saw thick plumes of smoke rising up from the scrubland by the track. We knew it was just Tomos burning the gorse back to maximize the grazing for the sheep. We got used to being unexpectedly delayed on our way to or from work when the lane was blocked by a herd of sheep, or we found ourselves behind Lewys and his slow-moving cows. The beasts would not be hurried, so we just had to sit and wait, and take the opportunity to chew the cud with Lewys.

In 2001, there was a major outbreak of foot and mouth disease in the UK. The prospect of our neighbours losing their livestock was awful. Because we had to cross Tomos' land to get to the cottage, he provided buckets of disinfectant for us to douse Buffy's wheels and our own wellies before entering or leaving the land. It was a worrying few weeks, but thankfully the disease was not detected on any of the local farms. However, it was a reminder of the precariousness of living off the land. Two years later, our own way of life and well-being were thrown into uncertainty when Geoff became ill, and we began to question the feasibility of our life on the hill.

19

Living on the hill and working in the city had always demanded stamina and the ability to work on multiple projects. I frequently felt like a juggler trying to keep lots of balls in the air simultaneously, anxious that one would fall if I took my eye off it for a second. We both had full teaching loads and were responsible for several undergraduate and postgraduate courses, which meant a hefty amount of admin work. A rise in student numbers and yet another change of management had translated into workload increases for everyone. We were working on a number of research projects and also trying to find time to keep in touch with family. We were making good progress at Tyn-y-Bryn but constantly aware of how much still needed to be done. Something had to give.

Geoff started feeling tired all the time—very tired. This was accompanied by feelings of weakness and light-headedness. Typically of Geoff, he carried on working. Some days he wasn't so bad, but the symptoms didn't improve. We had read about chronic fatigue syndrome, and the symptoms seemed to fit what Geoff was experiencing. We had still not registered with a family doctor in Wales, and anyway, Geoff was reluctant to seek conventional medical advice. Western medicine offers no cure for chronic fatigue and similar immune system disorders except for long-term anti-inflammatory medication, which Geoff was unwilling to take. Instead, he sought the advice of an acupuncturist.

A longstanding personal interest in alternative and complementary medicine had started to shape our research at the university. We were both fascinated by the ways in which personality and culture influence ways of thinking about the world, including science. We had become interested in the differences between Western and Eastern ways of conceptualizing the world.

Western thought is characterized by reductionism and emphasizes individual elements. Eastern thinking is more holistic and emphasizes the larger perspective. For example, the traditional way of giving one's address in Asian countries is to state the name of the country first, followed by the city and street, then the personal name last. You've guessed it: the opposite order is used in the West.

These different ways of thinking about the world inform the way science and medicine have developed in Eastern and Western countries. Western medicine excels in detailed study of the parts of systems, such as organs, cells, and genes, but struggles to fully understand systemic problems not connected with actual physical changes, such as chronic fatigue. Eastern medicine focuses on the energetics of the whole system, and so is better at addressing complex illnesses that require more individualized approaches. In fact, older, more traditional Western approaches to health and illness, such as herbal medicine, are also based on a holistic energetic model of the body, but this model has been lost with the rise of modern biomedicine.

After only one session with Xiao, an acupuncturist with a practice five minutes from the university, Geoff felt that his limbs were flooded with energy. With regular acupuncture treatments, he began to improve, although it was a lengthy recovery. The long working days followed by the lengthy commute were taking their toll on both of us. The motorway traffic increased yearly, and it wasn't unusual for us to be getting home at 8 or 9 p.m. some evenings if there had been roadworks or an accident on the motorway. We reasoned that if we could reduce our travelling by having somewhere to stay nearer work during the week it would help to conserve both our energy and our finances.

Unfortunately we couldn't afford to rent a flat or even a room in the city. Luckily, our family came to the rescue. My parents offered us the use of a sofabed. And Geoff's mother had a caravan near Chester which she was happy for us to use after work.

With somewhere to stay in the city, the working week became less frenetic. On Sunday evenings, we packed everything we would need for two days away. We drove to work early on Monday morning, stayed at either my parents' house or the caravan on Monday night, then drove home on Tuesday evening. The whole process was repeated on Thursday mornings. We were usually able to work at home on Wednesdays, writing or marking assignments. The new arrangement was easier and cut down our commute. However, although we were grateful for somewhere to stay, and nice as it was to spend some time with family, the new arrangement created its own tensions and challenges.

In *Hovel in the Hills*, Elizabeth West describes how she and Alan sometimes had to travel to the city to find work, leaving their home and garden for weeks at a time. I remember reading her account and thinking that at least we would never have to do the same to make ends meet, because we already had paid employment. But here we were, leading part-nomadic lives and spending most of our week in the city again. Our joy at escaping the system had been premature. It was true that compared with the Wests, we spent a lot less time away from home, but we constantly felt homesick for Tyn-y-Bryn and our lonely hillside. Enveloped in the centrally heated warmth of my parents' house, we missed the crackle of the fire and the smell of woodsmoke in the cold night air. We lay awake listening to the traffic and the garden birds, who, confused by the glare of the street lights, sang through the night, and we wondered if our barn owl was out hunting on the hill.

Staying at the caravan was quieter, but astonishingly cold. Like Tyn-y-Bryn, the caravan needed to be heated and lived in to remain warm in the winter, but unlike the cottage, the caravan's metal shell meant that it lost all heat overnight. Early morning starts at the caravan were therefore as frigid as those at the cottage. We grew to dread what we called the 'steaming sheets' experience at the caravan. Unfortunately, this is not as erotic as it sounds. It describes the feel of getting into a bed of damp sheets warmed only by hot water bottles and lying there until your body steams off the damp coolness and you fall into an uneasy sleep broken by dreams of warm cottage firesides.

My parents lived in a modern house on a housing estate. The fitted carpets and double glazing made us feel claustrophobic, and the presence of neighbours created a longing for the peace of the hillside. We were doing less travelling but spending more time in the city as a consequence. As a result, we felt uprooted and disconnected. The hill sustained us; we felt that we belonged to the land. Now we were spending more time away from home, we felt like we didn't belong anywhere. The dream of having more time and feeling more fulfilled seemed increasingly out of reach.

The Welsh term *hiraeth* does not translate directly into English but it comes closest to capturing our mood at that time. *Hiraeth* describes a feeling of homesickness tinged with nostalgia, or a yearning for something lost. We had yearned for a simpler life, an escape from the pressures of modern life. But it seemed it was harder than we thought to slip our chains.

Geoff's sessions with Xiao and our growing dissatisfaction prompted a new plan. We had become more and more interested in Chinese medicine, on both a personal and intellectual level. What better way to explore this interest further than by studying the discipline? We found a college that offered accredited acupuncture courses in York and applied for places. The course was part-time and held mostly at the weekends, so it could be completed while we were still working. There were some clinical practice days each year which occurred on week days, but the university permitted staff to take some days each year to pursue scholarly activity. Our line manager agreed that these days could be spent on acupuncture-related activity.

The acupuncture training was a big commitment in terms of time and money. But we had almost finishing paying off the loan on Tyn-y-Bryn. Moreover, being able to practice acupuncture was an additional skill that might provide an alternative income and a way out of academia. It was worth the extra work.

So our busy lives became even busier, but with a new impetus. Every other Saturday, we made the long drive from North Wales to York. Preparing for these weekends required almost military precision. We had to leave the cottage at 5.30 a.m. to be sure of reaching York in time for the first teaching session at 9 a.m. We took rolls and a flask of tea so that we could have a light breakfast in the car while on the move. If we had time, we stopped at a motorway service station for eggs on toast.

The weekends were gruelling but fascinating. As well as

lectures, there were sessions on acupuncture point location and massage techniques. We learnt about anatomy, the energetic pathways of the body, and patient–practitioner relationships. It was odd to be lecturers during the week and students at the weekend. And we brought plenty of work home with us; suddenly there were essays to write and textbooks to read on top of our usual university work.

Although much improved, Geoff still struggled at times with a lack of energy. During teaching weekends, he would often feel drained by the end of the morning and incredibly hungry. We would quickly have to find some food. Instead of just grabbing a damp sandwich, we would head to a vegetarian cafe not far from the college, where we would have a decent cooked meal to get us through the afternoon. Ironically, Geoff's struggles to maintain and improve his energy provided a real-life example of the concepts we were learning about on the course, such as the importance of the flow of qi, or energy, in health and illness, and the key role of eating well in nourishing this energy.

There is an oft-quoted saying in Chinese medicine: 'Eat breakfast like a king, lunch like a prince, and dinner like a pauper.' In other words, the biggest meals of the day should be breakfast and lunch. According to Chinese medicine, the digestive system functions best earlier in the day, so eating a large meal late at night leads to stagnation and digestive disharmony.

Like many people, we had been used to eating a very light breakfast and having only a sandwich for lunch (or sometimes missing lunch entirely if we were working hard in the garden). We now realized that this 'running on empty' habit wasn't good for long-term health and that the burnout Geoff was experiencing probably reflected these bad habits.

We began to think more deeply about how we managed

our energy and how we nourished ourselves. Geoff's illness had been a wake-up call. Now the extra study and travel demands of the training meant that we had to be careful about balancing work and rest. To improve our energy, we began to practice qigong and pay more attention to our eating patterns.

We received a useful lesson about the importance of a good breakfast from Dorothy, our landlady in York. We managed to book a room at Dorothy's most of the weekends we were in York. Dorothy was lively and a good raconteur. Following her retirement, she had turned two of the bedrooms in her pretty Georgian townhouse into bed and breakfast accommodation. She fussed over us and liked to try out new ideas for interesting breakfasts on us. From Dorothy's extensive menu choices, we had asked for porridge and a little toast. These she provided, together with a large range of jams, marmalades, and other condiments. However, she then evidently decided that we needed feeding up. The breakfasts started to expand.

'I've made you some scrambled eggs to go with your toast,' Dorothy would announce gaily, bustling into the dining room.

If she was feeling adventurous, the extras would be more elaborate.

'I made hash browns last night,' she would say, 'and I thought you would like some with your toast, eggs, and baked beans.'

We would smile politely and loosen our tight waistbands.

On one memorable day, Dorothy served us a large bowl of porridge each, followed by a substantial cooked vegetarian breakfast.

'I think I'm going to burst,' I whispered to Geoff.

'Shhh,' he said. 'Finish your coffee and let's go.'

But before we could hurry to our room, Dorothy came

sailing through the door bearing a large plate of chocolate croissants.

'I saw these in the patisserie yesterday,' she said. 'I just couldn't resist buying some for you!'

We never had the heart to tell Dorothy that we found her breakfasts daunting. She loved mothering us and she never charged us for the extra treats she provided. And it was curious how we quickly began to appreciate her huge breakfasts. Although we both felt full afterwards, by lunchtime we were ravenous. We realized the wisdom of the Chinese saying about eating breakfast like a king; a good breakfast, once one got used to it, boosted the digestive energy and kept you going all day. However, on those Sundays when we had a heavy physical session in the morning, such as massage, we had to beg Dorothy for mercy and insist on a lighter breakfast!

20

Our move to the hills of North Wales was an attempt to become more grounded, to connect with an older, more authentic way of thinking and living. Underlying the decision to train in acupuncture was the desire to extend this exploration into a more personal realm, to change our physical and mental states, not just our environment. And being versed in a traditional method of healing had another advantage. It provided another level of self-sufficiency because it meant that we could take care of each other rather than depending on the system for help.

However, although the acupuncture training had boosted our personal and intellectual development, it wasn't helping progress on the building work at Tyn-y-Bryn. Being away in York every other weekend meant that when we were at the cottage, we had to work extra hard to catch up.

One thing holding us back was the challenge of moving the huge stones we were going to use for the extension to the cottage. Some of the rocks were so massive Geoff couldn't move them by himself. And although the physical rigours of living at Tyn-y-Bryn, such as chopping wood and lifting heavy sacks of coal, had increased my physical strength, I wasn't exactly a weightlifter. We needed help.

We decided to look for a second-hand winch. This could be tied to something solid and used to lift the heaviest stones. It would speed up the building work and be a useful tool to keep at the cottage. After some searching, we came across a suitable winch advertised locally by a Mrs Jones. I called her on our mobile phone. The phone reception at the cottage was terrible so making a call involved climbing the hill behind the house and trying not to be blown over by the wind. It sounded like Mrs Jones had similar problems with reception because I caught only the occasional word of our conversation. She seemed to be in a phone box, and I was sure she mentioned sheep at one point. But we managed to agree on a time and date for us to call and see the winch.

Mrs Jones lived in the hills in a location that was more remote than our own. The combination of poor phone reception and her strong Welsh accent meant that I had gleaned only sketchy directions to her house. Nevertheless, we set off hopefully and were soon winding our way higher into the hills, along lanes that were almost deserted. On either side of the narrow road, the moorland stretched away for miles, broken only by scattered sheep. The landscape here could be bleak in winter but in summer the wide skies and scents of heather and gorse were exhilarating.

There was little in the way of landmarks in this wild expanse and we started to have doubts about our chances of finding Mrs Jones' house. Then, over the next rise we spotted a phone box. It looked incongruous in this wild moorland, as if it had just dropped from the sky. By the phone box stood an elderly woman who we hoped was Mrs Jones.

We pulled over by the phone box and got out. The woman peered at us short-sightedly, a little frown on her face.

'Um, Mrs Jones?' I asked tentatively. It occurred to me as I spoke that the woman could be just one of many Mrs

Jones in the area, so I hurriedly added, 'Are you the lady with the winch?'

The woman looked wary but nodded briskly.

'I am.'

In this exposed spot, there was a strong wind. Mrs Jones was wearing an enormous Mackintosh coat which flapped wildly around her legs, giving her the appearance of some strange large bird. We apologized for being a little late. She waved away our apologies, her expression softening slightly.

'I'll just get my things,' she said. 'Then I'll show you the winch.'

She reached inside the phone box and retrieved a battered handbag, a thermos flask, and a mobile phone. It was then we noticed that there was no phone in the telephone box itself.

'The reception in the house is atrocious,' Mrs Jones explained, gesturing towards an old farmhouse and a ramshackle collection of outbuildings situated nearby. 'So I have to come out here and stand in the phone box when I make a call!'

She beckoned us abruptly and started to make her way towards an old yellow estate car that was parked near the phone box.

'They keep saying they're going to come and take the phone box away,' she grumbled. 'But I won't let them! Where else am I supposed to stand to make a call when it's raining?'

We mumbled our sympathy.

'The winch is in the car,' she announced.

It wasn't the only thing that was in the car. In the front passenger seat sat a small boy. In the back of the car, where the seats should have been, was a large sheep. It looked unfazed by the arrangement and was chewing the cud contentedly. The window was down and as we approached, the sheep stuck its head out and regarded us carefully. Mrs Jones inclined her head towards the boy.

'My grandson,' she explained.

We nodded politely. She didn't mention the sheep and we didn't dare ask.

Mrs Jones' winch was just what we were looking for and we bought it on the spot. However, progress on the extension remained slow. The weather took a definite turn for the worse that year, with wild winds and lots of heavy rain. The worst storms always seemed to occur on the weekends we were at Tyn-y-Bryn, making building work and even gardening impossible.

The changing weather also began to make travelling difficult. One day, we reached the woods to find the track completely blocked. Heavy winds during the night had brought down a tall pine tree, which had fallen across the track. We parked Buffy on the track and Geoff walked back to the cottage to collect the chainsaw. We spent the next two hours cutting off tree branches and hauling them off the path to clear a way through for Buffy. It was a Saturday and we were heading to York for a training weekend. By the time we eventually got there, the morning sessions were practically over.

A few weeks later, three days of heavy rain caused major flooding and the closure of the Llanrwst road. We had to get to work so decided to take one of the smaller roads across the hills. We managed to get to Abergele with no problem, only to find a huge pool of water barring our way. With her off-road tyres, Buffy was usually able to cope with these kinds of situations. So we started to drive slowly through the water, confident of getting through. However, just when we thought we had passed the deepest point, the water seemed to suddenly get even deeper. A man walking his dog by the side of the road paused to watch and then began waving frantically at us to stop. We decided to play it safe and reversed Buffy back onto dry land. We had no choice but to turn around and go home, and to call the university to tell them we were unable to get to work.

The wild weather that year took its toll on our little homestead. Over the Christmas holiday, the wind blew so hard that we hardly slept for three days. We lay awake listening to the hundred mile an hour gusts rattling the slates on the roof and the wind turbine emitting the high-pitched wail it made when the wind was especially strong. At some point in the night the wail stopped and we fell into an uneasy sleep. The next morning we realized why the turbine had gone quiet: it had stopped completely. Despite the weather still being gusty that day, the turbine didn't move. It appeared to be broken. Luckily, it was still under guarantee but to get it fixed we had to take the pole down, dismantle the propeller, and package it up for shipping back to the turbine company in America.

The other casualty of the wind was the little shed, which housed the batteries and solar controller. An almighty gust one day pushed the shed off its base framework, leaving it leaning at an alarming angle. We had to move the batteries out and switch off the controller until we could fix it. Mrs Jones' winch was no good, as the shed was too big. Ten men could perhaps have pushed it back onto its base, but the two of us stood no chance. We began to think we would have to dismantle the shed and rebuild it onto the base. Then Geoff had the idea of using the car jack from Buffy to raise the end of the shed. It seemed an unlikely solution but it worked. Apart from some minor damage, the shed was fine, and relieved, we were able to reassemble the solar setup and switch the power back on.

The one thing that kept us positive that year was the fact that we had almost paid off Tyn-y-Bryn. The cottage may have been small and slightly ramshackle in places but it was finally ours and we were mortgage free. The completion of our loan also meant that we would be substantially better off each month. Satisfying at it would have been to splurge on spending, we decided instead to find a way to invest the extra money.

After much discussion we decided to buy another house. Although it seemed crazy to take on a mortgage when we had just paid off Tyn-y-Bryn, the difficulties with the weather and the increasing amount of time we were spending away from home meant that we badly needed somewhere to stay nearer to civilization. We reasoned that if we had a base in the city, we could stay there if it looked like we might get stranded at the cottage because of bad weather. It would also make it easier to get to York. The long drive back to Wales on Sunday evenings wasn't getting any easier. And although we were enjoying the acupuncture course, we often felt disoriented. On more than one occasion, I woke up in the morning with the odd feeling of not knowing where I was: was I at home in the cottage, at Dorothy's in York, at my parents' house, or at Geoff's mum's caravan? As I lay there in half-darkness, groggy with sleep, I usually managed to work out where I was by noting where the light was coming from. A soft light coming from my left, together with a deep peaceful stillness, meant that I was at the cottage and could relax.

There was another reason why owning a house in the city began to seem more attractive. Our weekends in York had, shall we say, opened our eyes to some of the charms of a big city. Without a doubt, we loved the peace and beauty of the hillside and had no desire to leave our rural haven. But there was something seductive about the energy of a large vibrant city that we could appreciate after living in the countryside for so long. And there were things about Liverpool that we missed: the museums and art galleries, the huge choice of restaurants, and the cosmopolitan nature of that huge urban melting pot.

We already felt like we leading a double life, working and training in the city and then racing back to the country to relax. Only we were usually so exhausted when we got to the cottage that we couldn't always appreciate being there. Having a bolthole in the city would simplify our lives and reduce the amount of commuting we had to do.

So we went to see a mortgage broker and started searching for suitable properties within striking distance of work. We had decided to look for a property that could generate some rental income. After all, we would only be there for some of the week so it made sense to have tenants there who could look after the place. But the search proved frustrating. We gave up on one estate agent who insisted on sending us details of expensive dockside apartments, despite explaining to her that we weren't millionaires. Another estate agent almost convinced us to buy a huge rambling house that was both cheap and of historic interest, until we found out that the house was practically next to the airport.

Eventually, we found a house that seemed ideal. It needed a lot of renovation but it had large bedrooms, big bay windows, and a small garden. Best of all, the large attic had been converted into a bedsit containing a large living and sleeping area, a small kitchen, and a shower room. This was exactly what we were looking for. The bedsit would provide us with a private living space and we could rent out the other bedrooms.

But first, there was a lot of renovation work to do. We wanted to do the work ourselves rather than buy someone in but it quickly became apparent that this would be impossible. Not only did the roof need work, but the house needed rewiring and new kitchens and bathrooms.

Strangely, it proved harder to find a builder than it had been to find the right house. It seemed that everyone in Liverpool was renovating their homes that year. But after much searching, we managed to secure the services of Mick, a capable but shifty character with a fondness for consuming takeout pizzas and lager during working hours.

We had been impressed by Mick's artfully designed and professional-looking website. However, when he turned up, the man himself didn't inspire confidence. He extended a filthy hand for Geoff to shake and leered at me.

'I can't start until next week,' he announced, 'but I'll have a look at the place now and give you a quote. Oh, and I'll need some money today.'

He grinned lopsidedly, showing a mouth with several missing teeth. We followed him round the house as he appraised, poked, and shook his head at various features. He looked cheery when we told him we wanted to replace the kitchens and bathrooms.

'Yeah, good idea,' he nodded. 'Rip 'em out.'

We got the impression that Mick's forte was demolition rather than reconstruction, which was rather worrying.

'For this one,' he said, gesturing round the main bathroom, 'I can get hold of new fittings for, oh, maybe four hundred. And it will only cost five hundred for the labour.'

'But that's more than the cost of the bathroom itself!' Geoff said.

'Okay, okay, don't get worked up, mate,' Mick said. 'Maybe it won't be as much as that.' He turned to me and grinned. 'Your hubby's a worrier!' he said.

We exchanged glances. We suspected that Mick was pulling random figures out of his head.

'We need a proper itemized quote before we can agree to

the work,' Geoff explained.

'Oh aye,' Mick said. 'The wife'll do that. It's one of her jobs.' He leered at me again.

After a breakneck tour of the place, Mick left, announcing that he had to meet one of his 'lads' in the pub. He promised to return with the lads the following week to start work. We had refused to give him any money until we had seen his detailed quote for the work and he had turned quite grumpy. However, as we were showing him out, he was hailed by the man who lived in the house directly opposite ours, who sauntered across the road for a chat. We knew nobody in the neighbourhood yet, but the man obviously knew Mick. After a few minutes of small talk, our neighbour got in his Mercedes and drove away.

'Do you know him well?' Mick asked.

I shook my head. 'First time we've spoken to him.'

Mick leaned in close to us and said conspiratorially, 'He's a gangster, that one.'

We looked at him disbelievingly.

'It's true,' he insisted. 'I didn't know he lived round here now.' Then he grinned at us happily. 'Oh, I'll tell you some stories about him next week,' he said. 'Just you wait!'

And he was gone, his ancient white van rattling dangerously up the road. We went inside, exhausted, and wondered what we taken on.

21

They say that moving house is one of the most stressful things you can do. However, we can confidently say that moving into a cottage with no electricity or running water on a dark winter's night was as nothing to the stress of managing the building work on our new Liverpool home, which we called the Halfway House. Over the next few months, we did battle on an almost daily basis with Mick and his band of adolescent assistants.

Despite having agreed a price for the renovation, Mick managed to swindle us at almost every stage of the project. For example, we had asked him to keep the old roof slates when he replaced the roof because we knew we could sell them for a good price. When he had finished the roof he showed us the salvaged slates, which he had stored in the old shed in the garden.

'But there aren't many slates here,' Geoff pointed out. 'Where are the rest?'

'Oh, they all got damaged when we took them off the roof,' Mick said vaguely. He looked distinctly shifty.

'So how come these ones didn't get damaged?' Geoff asked.

Mick shrugged. 'Maybe these were just tougher,' he

suggested. 'A bit like me!' He flexed his biceps and gave us a toothless smile.

We gave up. We knew he had probably pilfered most of the slates and sold them but we had no proof.

Then there was the time he sent two of his lads round to finish tiling the kitchen. To our dismay, they were both students of ours. We liked to keep our work and home life separate and weren't keen on the students knowing where we lived. However, it couldn't be helped. When they had finished the tiling, which we couldn't help noticing was as mediocre as their academic work, they asked for payment.

'But we've already given Mick the money for the tiling!' Geoff said.

The students protested that Mick had told them we would pay them directly. We refused. They sulked. Eventually we sent them away to sort the issue out with Mick. When we tackled him about it, Mick brushed off the issue.

'We gave you the money up front for all the tiling,' Geoff said.

Mick shrugged. 'Forgot,' he said.

We were never sure whether Mick was genuinely absent-minded or just plain devious. Certainly he seemed to lead a full life. He played rugby every weekend (hence the missing teeth). And then there was his wife.

'She has needs,' he explained to Geoff one day.

'Needs?' Geoff replied hesitantly, reluctant to be drawn into this conversation.

'Yes,' Mick said. 'You know, *needs*. I have to go home and give her a good seeing to twice a day!'

'It's not funny' he protested, seeing Geoff's expression. 'I'm knackered!'

Mick's motley crew of lads also gave us cause for concern. One of his workers, Peter, was a quiet lad who always had a cheerful word or two when we met him. According to

Mick, however, this impression was deceptive. Peter was prone to bouts of extreme behaviour, he said.

'He worked with me on me last job,' Mick told us, 'and do you know what he did one day?'

We shook our heads. Each of Mick's stories was more preposterous than the last.

'Well, I only asked him to mix up some cement—we were fixing some roof tiles in place—and he went proper berserk! He stormed out, effing and blinding, and do you know where we found him ten minutes later?'

We didn't.

'On the roof, completely starkers!'

'Naked?'

Mick nodded. 'He climbed up there, took off all his clothes and threw them off the roof. In the end, we had to get the fire brigade in to get him down.'

'Do you think he's fit to work now?' I asked. 'Surely he needs some help with his, um, issues.'

'Nah,' Mick said, biting into his burger. 'He's right as rain now. Anyway, I need a good roofer so I can't let him go.'

He must have noticed our expressions because he said 'Don't worry. Me dad was a nutter so I know how to handle 'em. And I keep him off cement duty nowadays.'

Peter continued to be hard-working and peaceable throughout the project but we could never completely relax around him after Mick's revelations. We watched the poor boy like hawks, and every time he took off his sweatshirt or adjusted the waistband of his jeans we grew nervous. As an extra precaution, I put the number of the fire brigade on speed dial.

But eventually the building work was done. Although it wasn't to the highest standard, we were past caring. We just wanted rid of Mick. When he offered to take on the task of decorating the whole house, we declined. We didn't think we could stand the financial or mental strain of working with him again.

We decorated and furnished the bedsit in the attic first, so that we could begin staying over on week nights. The rest of the house would have to wait. Having somewhere to stay close to work made a big difference to our lives. Because we were able to work longer hours at the university, we didn't have to take as much work home with us when we did escape to Tyn-y-Bryn. And acupuncture weekends were less tiring because we had less distance to drive. But loading up Buffy for two days in the city was now a major task. As well as our work and (sometimes) acupuncture gear, we packed fresh vegetables from the garden and two days supply of spring water. Our soft spring water was gentle on the skin and excellent to drink. We had no choice but to wash in the chlorinated city water, but we refused to drink it.

By that time, the only cat we still had at the cottage was Bibby. We worried about him while we were away but he seemed quite content on the hill. Before we left for each two-day stint we left him a bowl of tinned cat food, which he always ate immediately, and two days worth of cat biscuits. We had bought one of those electronic pet feeders that supposedly permit staggered feeding times. We filled the different sections of the feeder, which we called the Bibtronic, with cat biscuits, and programmed the timer so that Bibby would have access to a new pile of biscuits twice a day. However, Bibby's timing was appalling and he always seemed to miss the opening of a new section of the Bibtronic, probably because he was off trekking over the hillside worrying the endangered water voles. Consequently, we usually returned after two days to a furious and hungry cat and a Bibtronic full of stale cat biscuits.

Although we were impatient to rent out some rooms,

decorating and furnishing the house, as well as fixing all the little problems Mick had left, was time-consuming and had to be fitted in after work. We hoped to be able to let out rooms to professional people, as the house was attractive and the neighbourhood was, with one exception, generally quiet. Unfortunately, that exception was the house next door.

Our house was semi-detached so we were joined to the home of our loutish next door neighbours. With characteristic wit, Mick had named the family next door the Clampetts, after the rough hillbilly family in a 1960s American television series. They were a family of four: Billy, Tracey, and their children Chelsea and Little Billy. The Clampetts weren't bad people, but they were noisy, brash, and not entirely trustworthy. At one time, Tracey's father had owned both their house and our own, and we always felt that the Clampetts still considered our house to be theirs by rights. When the seller of our house had moved out, he had left the keys with the Clampetts. By the time we picked up the keys, we noticed that several fixtures and fittings that the seller had left for us had disappeared. We suspected that they had been spirited away next door, but the Clampetts vehemently denied this.

After an initially rocky start, our relationship with the Clampetts improved slightly. If we were working in the front garden, Tracey would sometimes stand at their front door in her bathrobe, smoking and chatting to us. Big Billy only grunted at us at first. We had argued with him over what was to happen to the two chimneys that the houses shared. Mick had advised us that they were not in good repair and should be lowered and capped. We suggested to Big Billy that we should arrange to have this work done and pay for it jointly. He refused point-blank.

'But the chimneys are dangerous,' Geoff pointed out.

'They might fall on someone.'

'I don't care,' Billy had retorted. 'We don't want them fixed. It would ruin the look of the house.'

We were mystified. We hadn't thought of Big Billy as being particularly interested in architecture, and the Clampetts seemed anything but houseproud. However, the mystery was solved one day after Geoff had again raised the chimney issue with Big Billy.

'We really think the chimneys need to be sorted,' Geoff had said. 'They could fall down at any time.'

Big Billy had disagreed forcefully, finishing by saying, 'Well, you do what you like with them. But you'll get no money from me!'

As it wasn't an expensive job, we went ahead and paid to have the chimneys fixed. After the job was done, when there was no chance of us asking him for money, Big Billy became quite chatty.

We felt a little sorry for the Clampett kids. Seventeen and heavily pregnant, Chelsea was engaged to an angry youth who Billy and Tracey disapproved of. Chelsea's beau would sometimes turn up late at night and shout impassioned speeches full of expletives up at her bedroom window.

Little Billy had the infuriating habit of standing at the gate and kicking his football against our front door. We suspected he did it for attention because whenever we opened the door to tell him off he tried to engage us in conversation.

One day, he said to Geoff, 'You're a doctor aren't you? I've got problems with me skin.'

'I'm not that kind of doctor,' Geoff said.

'But look,' Little Billy persisted, 'Look at these spots!'

'Mmm. You have got quite a lot, haven't you?'

'And look at me mouth ulcers,' Billy said, pulling his lower lip down. 'What can I do about them?'

'Try eating less chips,' Geoff said.

One day, I was upstairs painting one of the bedrooms when Geoff called me downstairs. He pointed out of the front room window.

'Look at that.'

Parked outside the Clampetts' house was a taxi. Little Billy and another boy who lived nearby went for extra maths lessons each week, and they were picked up by the same taxi firm. However, today their taxi didn't seem to be going anywhere. Instead, it was rocking quite violently from side to side.

'What is it?' I asked Geoff. 'Is there an earth tremor or something?'

Just then the taxi driver emerged, ran down the Clampetts' path, and hammered on their front door. The next thing we knew, Tracey and Big Billy were hauling Little Billy and his friend out of the back seat of the taxi and thwacking them both round the head. The two boys had obviously decided to have a punch up before their maths lesson. From what we could see, it took some persuasion from Big Billy to get the taxi driver back in the car with the little louts.

The small garden we inherited at the Halfway House was full of weeds and broken paving stones. We cleared the weeds and Geoff laid a new patio. There was not enough space for a greenhouse, but the first summer we were there we planted tomatoes and courgettes in the beds. The brick wall surrounding the garden gave some warmth and shelter so Geoff, who was constantly saving seeds, planted out a small apricot tree he had grown from a stone saved from a particularly nice apricot we had eaten.

Our gardening endeavours were often carried out under the scrutiny of Little Billy. Our shed shared a common wall with next door's shed so defying Tracey's feeble protests, Billy would often scramble onto the shed roofs to watch us.

One day, Geoff shouted to Little Billy, 'Come down.'

The kid shook his head and looked sulky.

'Come down,' Geoff repeated. 'It's okay, I just want to give you something.'

Little Billy clamboured down and made his way hesitantly to where Geoff was working in the vegetable bed.

'Hold your hands out,' Geoff instructed. He picked a good pile of little cherry tomatoes and piled them into Little Billy's open hands.

'I don't like tomatoes,' Billy said.

'I bet you'll like these ones,' Geoff said.

Little Billy popped a tomato into his mouth and chewed thoughtfully.

'They're nice,' he said. 'They're like sweets.'

'Go to the kitchen door,' Geoff said, 'and ask Marie to put them in a bag for you to take home.'

A day or two later, we bumped into Chelsea as we were leaving for work.

'Me dad says to thank you for the tomatoes,' she said. 'They're lovely!'

'Glad you liked them,' Geoff said.

'I'm going to grow some of my own next year,' she said, a determined look on her face. 'And maybe some of those lettucey things you've got in your garden!'

We were surprised but pleased at the girl's sudden interest in gardening and promised her some veg seeds before the next growing season.

One of the bedrooms we had yet to decorate was south facing and had a large window. To maximize food production, we turned it into a growing room where we could raise seeds before planting out. We had two old paste tables which we covered with seed trays and propagators. Some of the seedlings we raised we took back to the cottage to plant out there.

The worsening weather was making gardening on the hill increasingly difficult. The old polytunnel cover had been patched so often that it was more tape than plastic. We ordered a new cover and spent a weekend strengthening the polytunnel framework and putting the new cover on. Three weeks later a strong gale tore the cover beyond repair and threw it across the garden. As we couldn't afford to buy another one, we had to depend on our makeshift growing room in the Halfway House for sowing that year.

The storms that year also finished off the wind turbine. We had sent it to America to be repaired and the manufacturer expressed astonishment that the wind had broken it, as it was one of their most robust models. However, they repaired it free of charge and sent it back. Literally one week after we reinstalled the turbine, a heavy gale damaged it again. We gave up. Obviously our wild weather was too much for the turbine which, though heavy duty, was a domestic rather than an industrial model. We decided to chalk the turbine episode up to experience and concentrate on solar power.

The changing weather continued to make access to Tyn-y-Bryn difficult at times. One rainy, windy Friday evening, we drove back to Wales, stopping off at the supermarket to buy provisions for the weekend. We got halfway up the track through the woods and had to brake sharply. A live electrical cable had fallen across the track, obviously brought down by the wind. The cable had hit and burnt a tree at the edge of the track and the flames had spread to some nearby bushes. We considered calling the fire brigade but as we watched, the rain grew heavier and the flames died out, leaving the bushes smouldering in the dusk. We couldn't drive across the cable so, with difficulty, we reversed Buffy back down the track.

We had to leave Buffy parked at the bottom of the track

that night and struggle up the hill on foot with our work bags and shopping bags. As we plodded up through the rain-soaked wood, we thought of Beti and Will, our neighbours who lived at the bottom of the hill. With the power out, they would be fretting that night, searching in cupboards for candles and bemoaning the lack of central heating. We thought with satisfaction of our primitive but cozy cottage. When we got home, we would light the stove and hang our clothes in front of the fire to dry. Our small off-grid system would be unaffected by the power cut. We would switch on our little 12-volt lights in the kitchen and start preparing dinner. With no central heating system to fuss over, after dinner we would fill our hot water bottles and take them up to bed, snuggling down under a pile of woollen blankets to hide from the storm.

22

It was August and I was sat in Buffy outside a farmhouse near Llanrwst. I was reading a book on qigong and trying to ignore the howling of the strong winds buffeting the Jeep. I had switched off the windscreen wipers because they were no match for the torrential rain that streamed down the windscreen. I was waiting for Geoff, who was inside the house giving an acupuncture treatment to one of his new patients.

We had finished our training and were now qualified acupuncture practitioners. Because of the difficult access, we couldn't practice from Tyn-y-Bryn, so had decided to provide a mobile service. Equipped with a portable treatment bed and a small supply of needles, we could provide weekend treatments to anyone within driving distance.

Only it wasn't that simple of course. Since we had started practicing barely a month ago, the weather had been apocalyptic. The problems we had encountered trying to visit our patients, all of who lived in very rural locations, included fallen trees, flooding, and power cuts. The patient Geoff was currently treating, the owner of the farmhouse, had only just repaired her track, part of which had been washed away by heavy rain.

I thought I saw a blur of movement through the car window and switched on the wipers. Geoff had finished the session and was struggling to the car with the treatment bed. I put my book down and went to help. In driving rain, we stashed the bed into Buffy's boot and flung ourselves into the front seats, switching on the heater. We headed down the track, driving through streams of water that were rapidly becoming little torrents. We suspected that the repairs to the track would be short-lived.

It was becoming clear that what we really needed was a base in town that we could use as a clinic. So we called in at the estate agents to see if Gavin could help. The good news was that there were lots of properties for rent in Llanrwst. The bad news was that only one was anywhere near our price range. We agreed to go and view it.

Gavin was vague about the price because apparently there were actually three potential rental spaces at the property, which was a small shop in the centre of town that had recently been totally refurbished. It even had a tiny garden. One of the spaces to let was the ground floor of the shop. At first viewing, it was impressive, with the smell of new carpets and freshly painted walls. But it consisted of only one smallish room. To create a private treatment room, a separate space would have to be partitioned off from the door. And it was five hundred pounds a month, way above our budget.

'Not to worry,' Gavin said. 'There's a very nice room upstairs, which is actually cheaper.'

We gingerly climbed the stairs. I say gingerly because the stairs were so steep they were almost vertical. Gavin was not the most agile of men and he hung onto the handrail for dear life. The room was indeed very nice, with a large skylight and even a sink. It could have made a good treatment room if it hadn't been for that lethal staircase.

Descending the stairs was even more alarming; you had to duck sharply to avoid a low overhang at the top of the stairs before attempting the vertiginous return journey. We reluctantly concluded that any benefits our patients might have gained from an acupuncture treatment would likely be removed when they broke their necks going downstairs.

Gavin looked at his notes.

'It says here that there's an outbuilding at the bottom of the garden which is available for rent. Maybe that will be suitable?'

Hopefully, we followed Gavin into the garden. A clinic in a garden would be nice; we pictured a peaceful healing space surrounded by herbs and flowers.

Gavin halted outside a small structure at the bottom of the garden. 'Here we are. Um ... I think it has a lot of potential.'

We stared at the 'outbuilding'.

'Gavin, it's a shed,' Geoff pointed out.

'Well ... more like a summerhouse or a garden room maybe,' Gavin said.

'No, it's definitely a shed,' Geoff insisted.

'Mmm.' Gavin had the grace to look embarrassed. 'Maybe it could be improved in some way?'

'Only by pulling it down,' Geoff said.

As we were not prepared to treat our patients in a damp shed, we were forced to give up the search for clinic premises. The modest wage we would make from acupuncture would not, it seemed, even cover the cost of rent.

We decided to put the idea of starting a clinic on hold and take a holiday to celebrate finishing the acupuncture course. We had some friends who lived in mid-Wales, so we drove down for a brief visit before continuing to Tenby, where we had booked to stay for a few days. On the way to

Tenby, we stopped for lunch in Machynlleth, the ancient capital of Wales and home to the Centre for Alternative Technology, which we were fond of visiting when we could.

A brilliant blue sky had slowly darkened as we had driven south, and by the time we reached the town the heavens had opened. We threw on raincoats and raced to the nearest cafe. There, over Earl Grey tea and huge slices of carrot cake, we wondered whether we had chosen the wettest week of the year to go on holiday.

However, by the time we reached Tenby the sun was blazing on streets that glistened wet from the recent downpours, and it continued to blaze all week. We visited the tiny cathedral city of St Davids and walked down its hot little streets, past surf shops and pavement cafes. In Tenby, we ate dinner one night on a restaurant terrace overlooking the sea and felt ourselves start to unwind. If only the weather was like this more of the time!

As holidays do, the week sped by and we were soon driving north again, hoping that the glorious weather would follow us back to the hill. It didn't. The sunshine we had enjoyed all week evidently had not reached North Wales, and we drove back through a landscape that showed the signs of a recent deluge. We glanced over the hedgerows at flooded fields and were repeatedly held up at roadworks, as sections of road were flooded or under repair.

To extend the holiday a little, we had decided to call at the village of Portmeirion, which was built by the architect Sir Clough Williams-Ellis on a hillside overlooking the River Dwyryd. Portmeirion is a baroque fantasy filled with architectural follies and playful landscape features. Its pastel-coloured houses, terracotta roof tiles, and Italianate courtyards were inspired by the Italian Riviera village of Portofino.

We usually loved the Riviera atmosphere of Portmeirion,

but on that day it seemed to have an air of melancholy. Its pink and yellow walls and terracotta roofs were damp with algae and the statues stood around disconsolately amongst the dripping vegetation. Workers were busy painting and cleaning up areas that had been affected by the bad weather, an uncomfortable reminder of the ongoing work on the cottage waiting for us when we got home.

Following our brief holiday, we reluctantly flung ourselves back into the craziness of academia. University life had been particularly stressful over the last few months. Like our colleagues, we had been groaning under the strain of recent rapid changes to the structure of teaching and research. And there were rumours of redundancies. Worst of all, there was a growing trend in the university sector to steer research towards those topics that would bring in money. Research areas that were not so lucrative were marginalized, and any criticism of this trend was discouraged. We both felt that the changes were anathema to the spirit of open scientific enquiry and free speech, which are the basis of the concept of a university. We began to wonder how long we could stay in academia.

The autumn weather did nothing to improve our mood. A strange cold breeze had haunted the hillside for the last three years and now seemed to have followed us to the city. The breeze penetrated the shelter of the little walled garden of the Halfway House and one night a strong wind blew several slates off the roof.

We found ourselves spending more and more time at the Halfway House. One Friday evening, we drove home to Wales through falling snow. The roads in the valley had only a light dusting of sleet, but up in the village thick snowdrifts lay up against the hedgerows and the sharp bend in the road by the old elm tree was perilously icy.

We got as far as the bottom of the track but then Buffy's wheels started to skid. After half an hour, we gave up. The ice was thick and we just couldn't get a purchase on the road surface.

We parked Buffy up and got out. The air was freezing. The prospect of carrying all our baggage up through thick snow to the cottage wasn't appealing. The snow was falling faster now; if it continued to snow all weekend, we might get snowed in and be unable to get to work the following week. The sensible solution was to turn round and head straight back to the Halfway House but we couldn't leave Bibby without food. And after being away for two days we wanted to check that all was well at the cottage. So we strapped on head torches and trekked up the hill, trying not to twist an ankle in the deep ruts in the track, which were now hidden by the snow.

Bibby had clearly been planning a cozy evening in front of the fire and was intensely annoyed at being placed in his cat box and carried down to the Jeep through thick snow. He howled in protest all the way back to Liverpool.

Over the next few months, we spent more time at the Halfway House than at Tyn-y-Bryn. Partly this was because we were trying desperately to finish the final jobs on the house before renting out rooms. But it was also because of a sneaking reluctance to spend the winter weekends at the cottage. In Gwyn's time, the cottage would always have been full of people and the stove would have been lit all the time. A stone house on a damp hillside must be lived in to stay warm and dry. Now we were spending more time away from the hill, Tyn-y-Bryn was becoming colder and damper all the time. Perhaps the cold was seeping into our bones, because it seemed harder to get the place feeling warm, especially at night. It didn't help that we had both had awful bouts of flu that winter. We felt guilty, and we missed the hill terribly, but most weekends all we wanted to do after work was to flee back to the Halfway House and put the central heating on.

Things came to a head one Saturday. We had driven back to the cottage the previous evening. The usual two-hour journey had taken four and half hours because of an accident on the motorway. It had been a particularly trying week at work and the weather had been appalling. We had got drenched every morning just sprinting across the campus from the car to the office. We both felt like we were getting colds (literally 'under the weather'!) and were especially grumpy that Saturday morning as we reluctantly headed out to do some shopping.

The rain hammered down as we raced down the track to Buffy. Dripping, we clamboured into the Jeep and switched the heater on full. The rain had eased off a little by the time we got to the gate by the woods, but as Geoff climbed out to open the gate another downpour started. As Geoff was fastening the gate behind us, the wind whipped his raincoat hood off. By the time he had struggled with the heavy old padlock on the gate and climbed back in the car, his raincoat hood was half full of water and little rivulets of rain ran down his face.

'That's it!' he fumed, as he struggled to take off his coat. 'I've had enough! I don't think I can take much more of this!'

I helped him off with his coat, and considered whether or not to voice the guilty thought that had been in my mind for the last few weeks. The lifestyle we had chosen wasn't easy and it wasn't unusual for us to experience moments of frustration. But I hadn't seen Geoff like this before.

'Maybe we should think about moving,' I said quietly. 'Perhaps abroad.'

The speed of his reply surprised me. 'Maybe we should,'

he said.

We looked at each other, shocked.

We said little on the drive into Llandudno. The enormity of the prospect of leaving Tyn-y-Bryn and our hill seemed to hang in the air between us, rendering us both silent and thoughtful.

We hurried round the supermarket, our minds elsewhere. Driving past the cinema on the way out of Llandudno, we caught sight of a billboard advertising the film *Mamma Mia*, which was currently showing. Musicals weren't our thing but we had seen a trailer for the film and its scenes of brilliant blue skies and white sandy beaches had seemed rather appealing after weeks of storms.

'Let's go and see it,' Geoff said suddenly.

'What?'

'That film, *Mamma Mia*. Let's go and see it now.'

'But we were planning to work on the outbuilding this afternoon,' I said.

'In this?' Geoff gestured through the windscreen at the rain. 'By the look of that sky, the rain isn't going to let up any time soon. We can't get anything done in this. Besides, I need some sunshine!'

I knew what he meant. So, uncharacteristically, we took the afternoon off and sat in the cinema in our damp clothes gazing at a screen filled with images of azure Greek skies, sun-drenched hillsides, and whitewashed houses covered with scarlet bougainvillea.

On the way back, we called in at a newsagents and bought a stack of magazines about moving to various European countries.

That evening, over a bottle of wine in front of the fire, we did our research. The magazine pictures of Mediterranean vistas and exotic villas were enticing, but our mood was serious. Never before had we felt any doubts about living on the hill, or had any desire to leave Wales. It was possible that this was just a blip, an aberration brought on by bad weather and overwork. But we had to find out, one way or the other. The magazines would be a test, a way of exploring our feelings and examining the pros and cons of living abroad.

Watching the film had stirred memories of a long-ago holiday I had enjoyed in Greece. But the fierce heat of Greek summers worried us. We wanted to be able to grow things and have an active lifestyle all year round.

'What about France?' I asked Geoff, gazing at an image of lavender fields on a hill in Provence.

'Too expensive,' he said. 'Except in the north. Where it's too wet.'

Spain was another obvious choice but it was already full of expats. In an odd way, we both felt that if we were going to take the plunge and move abroad, it had to be somewhere that felt foreign, not a British enclave in the sun.

'Italy looks nice,' I said, leafing through the *Living in Italy* magazine. The pictures of Tuscan vineyards were appealing. But Tuscany was out of our price range and neither of us had actually been to Italy. And Geoff had a different kind of objection.

'I couldn't do Italy. The Italians are massive extraverts.'

'That's probably a stereotype.'

'I know, but I wouldn't like to take the chance!'

He picked up the *Portugal* magazine. I had never been to Portugal, but Geoff had visited the Algarve before we met.

'I really warmed to the Portuguese people,' he said. 'They seem gentle and quite reserved. I think we'd feel at home there.'

I felt my stomach do a little lurch at his words. *Home.* Ten years ago, we had thought that the hillside and Tyn-y-Bryn were home, and always would be. Now we were less sure.

As much as we felt like traitors, sitting there in the cottage talking about abandoning the place, things had changed. The hillside felt different, more inhospitable. Or was it us that had changed? Maybe the battles at work and the battles with the weather had sapped our energy and we no longer had what it took to live in such a harsh environment. Or maybe we just wanted different things now.

I suddenly remembered the strange dream I had had on that first night at the cottage. My dream image of being safe in a tower on a beautiful hillside surrounded by the noise and stress of the city seemed now to make sense. We had run to North Wales to escape the pressures of the city and of work. But maybe there were some things you couldn't run from. We had been searching for an older way of life, inspired by our vision of a pre-modern idyll. But we weren't living in Gwyn's time any more. Times had changed and the world had moved on. There was no escaping that.

Or was there? We gazed at the pictures in the *Portugal* magazine of warmer hillsides and the blue blue sea, cobbled streets and medieval town squares. If the images could be believed, time seemed to have stood still in Portugal. By the end of the evening, an idea that had started as a vague possibility now seemed inevitable. The meaning of my dream all those years ago was now clear. The journey wasn't over.

EPILOGUE

The poet Rainer Maria Rilke wrote, 'Anxious, we keep longing for a foothold — we at times too young for what is old and too old for what has never been.' Maybe this is a good image for what the Welsh call *hiraeth*, a sense of yearning for a bygone time that was somehow simpler and more authentic. Those early years at Tyn-y-Bryn now seem like a dream. The weather had been kind to us then; the winters were crisp and clear and the summers long and hot. We had congratulated ourselves on moving to the mountains; if the climate was warming up, then we would be safe on our hillside with its cool breezes and myriad streams.

But then life had changed. The things we had come to take for granted—the academic careers, being able to live off the land, seasons that were predictable—no longer seemed so certain. What we had loved about Tyn-y-Bryn was that we were immersed in nature, attuned to the elements. But those elements had become increasingly harsh. The snowfall had become heavier, the winds stronger and more biting, the flooding a regular occurrence. Was it a failing in us, an inability to cope? Or had our time on that magical hillside come to a natural end? Whatever it was, we felt we had to uproot ourselves and move on.

I can remember still the feel of soft, damp grass under my feet as I walk from the cottage to the little wall by the holly tree. From this vantage point, I can see the storm clouds gathering.

'Fifteen minutes to rain!' we used to laugh, undaunted by the heavy skies.

From the shelter of the holly tree, I can study every curve and shadow of the Snowdonia mountain range. 'Our mountains,' we used to call them. And I can remember how, during those cold later years, a warm southerly breeze would occasionally blow in to touch the mountains. This rare visitor would carry different scents, softer airs. And we would turn our faces to greet it, breathe in, and dream of southern skies.

BIBLIOGRAPHY AND FURTHER READING

Abram, D. (1996). *The Spell of the Sensuous.* Vintage Books.

Bachelard, G. (1994). *The Poetics of Space.* (M. Jolas, Trans.). Beacon Press.

Bohm, D. (1996). *On Dialogue.* Routledge.

Borrow, J. (2009). *Wild Wales.* Bridge Books.

Cope, J. (2011). *The Modern Antiquarian.* Thorsons.

Hillman, J. (1976). *Revisioning Psychology.* Harper & Row.

Rilke, R. M. (1922). *The Sonnets to Orpheus.*
(See also his wonderful *Letters to a Young Poet* (1929)).

Seymour, J. (1976). *The Complete Book of Self-Sufficiency.* Faber & Faber.

Shepard, P. (1997). *The Others: How Animals Made Us Human.* Island Press.

The following books are specifically about North Wales.

West, E. (1978). *Hovel in the Hills.* Corgi.

West, E. (1981). *Garden in the Hills.* Corgi.
(Further adventures of the Wests.)

Corbett, J. (2004). *Castles in the Air.* Random House.
(Fascinating account of one couple's struggle to renovate a
castle in Llanrwst.)

Firbank, T. (1999). *I Bought a Mountain.* John Jones
Publishing.
(The trails and tribulations of a couple who bought a sheep
farm in Snowdonia in the 1930s.)

Hill, A. L. (1954). *Four Fields, Five Gates.* John Jones
Publishing.
(The experiences of three women who bought a cottage in
the mountains to renovate.)

DISCLAIMER

All the events in this book actually happened and all the characters are real. However, the names of people and houses have been changed for privacy.

CONTINUE THE JOURNEY...

If you enjoyed *Escape to the Hills*, come with us to Portugal in the sequel *Escape to the Sea*.

Available spring 2023

Printed in Great Britain
by Amazon

59267960R00116